BISHOP ALEXANDER MACDONELL
AND THE POLITICS OF
UPPER CANADA

BISHOP ALEXANDER MACDONELL AND THE POLITICS OF UPPER CANADA

J. E. REA

ONTARIO HISTORIAL SOCIETY
RESEARCH PUBLICATION No. 4
TORONTO 1974

Table of Contents

INTRODUCTION

Until 1963, when Gerald Craig published his study, Upper Canada: The Formative Years, 1791-1841, the Tories of Upper Canada had not received a very good press. Most historians of the period, writing in the Whig tradition, tended to cast them in the antagonistic role of obstructionists in the path of British North America's great constitutional achievement, Responsible Government. The Family Compact, as they became known pejoratively, was a tightly-knit, élitist group who entrenched themselves in power and ran the province to their own advantage.[1]

Craig substantially revised this view by pointing out that the goals of the Compact--their grand design for Upper Canada--were not unacceptable to many of the people of the province.[2] The Tories did, after all, win as many elections as the Reformers. The opinion of Craig has been supplemented and extended by S.F. Wise in two particular areas; a careful examination of the intellectual content of Upper Canadian Toryism, and the nature of the political system in which the Tory group

---

[1] Examples of this interpretation are manifold. Some of the more well-known are Charles Lindsey, The Life and Times of Wm. Lyon Mackenzie, 2 vols., (Toronto, 1862); J.C. Dent, The Story of the Upper Canadian Rebellion, 2 vols., (Toronto, 1885); W.S. Wallace, The Family Compact, (Toronto, 1915); Stephen Leacock, Mackenzie, Baldwin, Lafontaine, Hincks, (Toronto, 1926); E.C. Guillet, The Lives and Times of the Patriots, (Toronto, 1938); S.D. Clark, Movements of Political Protest in Canada, (Toronto, 1949).

[2] See infra, Chapter III.

at the capital was buttressed and sustained by smaller élite groups in various centres in the province.[3] It is within the context of the recent literature about Upper Canada and its conservative élite that the career of Alexander Macdonell, first Roman Catholic Bishop of the province, can best be evaluated.

Macdonell did not hold executive or administrative office in Upper Canada. He is, therefore, much less familiar than John Strachan or Egerton Ryerson, the two other leading churchmen of the period. It should be noted, as well, that it was only recently that the bulk of Macdonell's private papers was made available to researchers. There is now, however, ample evidence to suggest that the Bishop played a not insignificant role in moulding the polity and values of the province. This is especially true as it applies to the numerous Catholic inhabitants of Upper Canada, but his influence spread well beyond his own religious community.

Alexander Macdonell was never a member of the Family Compact in the full sense. Obviously, he could not concede the question of church establishment to Strachan and those of the Tory élite who supported the Archdeacon in his claims. On all other aspects, however, Macdonell shared the assumptions and cardinal tenets which underlay the Compact's concep-tion of Upper Canada and its future. Thus, they were natural allies,

---

[3]See especially, S.F. Wise, "Upper Canada and the Conservative Tradition", Profiles of a Province, Ontario Historical Society, (Toronto, 1967); "Tory Factionalism: Kingston Elections and Upper Canadian Politics, 1820-1836", Ontario History, LVII (1965); and "God's Peculiar Peoples", in W.L. Morton (ed.), The Shield of Achilles, (Toronto, 1968).

both politically and socially. This alliance was expressed by Macdonell's consistent support of the executive government and the willingness of the government, in turn, to accommodate the Bishop in matters of patronage and financial aid to his church. By following Macdonell's career, then, it is possible to examine in some detail the general implications in the recent work of Professors Craig and Wise.

Bishop Macdonell has never been considered in this light, as a practising "associate member" of the Family Compact, using the leverage of his position to serve the interests of the Catholic population and the ideological thrust of the Tory leadership of Upper Canada. The secondary sources on Macdonell's life are disappointing. There is only one of any importance, H.J. Somers, The Life and Times of the Honourable and Right Reverend Alexander Macdonell, submitted as a doctoral dissertation to The Catholic University of America and published in 1931. Father (now Monsignor) Somers devoted his study to Macdonell as clergyman, the pioneer builder of the church in the wilderness of Upper Canada. Much of the emphasis was placed on physical accomplishments, such as the number of priests, churches and schools; and the context was that of the missionary church rather than the polity of Upper Canada. Somers' work is well documented for the time but much new material has become available in recent years. The result was a largely uncritical view of Macdonell with little detailed appreciation of the mechanics and the ideology of Upper Canadian politics. Somers' book, like his Bishop, was a pioneering venture.

CHAPTER I

YEARS OF PREPARATION

I

On November 1, 1804, a Highland priest named Alexander Macdonell arrived in York, the capital of Upper Canada, to present his letters of introduction to Lieutenant General Peter Hunter, then the Lieutenant Governor of the Province. Macdonell was forty-two years of age at the time; but ahead of him lay many eventful and fruitful years in this newly established British colony. He would encounter his share, and more, of frustration and disappointment. His zeal for his people and his vigorous conservatism would embroil him in the political life of the province. He would be pilloried and praised; but, in the end, could reflect with some satisfaction on his accomplishments.

If he took pride, as he did, in the fact that the Catholic religion became securely established in Upper Canada, and that his own position was akin to a patriarchal dignity, he was scarcely conscious that an aggressive illiberality had occasionally marked his career. His self-righteousness was his armour, shielding him from the slings and arrows of criticism. Yet it narrowed his range of alternatives, made him inflexible and dogmatic and, to a marked degree, authoritarian.[1] In his own view,

---

[1] It will be indicated in this study that Macdonell was closed-minded in the classic sense, unable to make distinctions among opinions or ideas which were opposed to his own, and authority-oriented to an extreme. See Milton Rokeach, The Open and Closed Mind, (New York, 1960), Part 1.

1

however, Macdonell was steadfast in his devotion to Catholicism and Monarchy, and his success in Upper Canada sufficient testimony to the wisdom and efficacy of his commitment. His profound conservatism did not evolve as a result of his experiences in the Province, but was fully formed when he arrived. It was during his youth and early manhood that he developed those traits of character and predisposition that would distinguish his activities in maturity. It was in these formative years that his intellectual engagement with monarchical institutions, hierarchical social structure and advancement through the patronage system of the day was made.

II

Alexander Macdonell was born on July 17, 1762, near the shores of Loch Ness in Inverness-shire, Scotland.[2] His childhood and youth were passed among the Clan in Glengarry who had clung to their Catholicism despite the penal laws imposed by the British Parliament. Paradoxically, the young Macdonell apparently felt no conflict of loyalties. Clan Macdonell had supported Prince Charlie in 1745 and had suffered heavily.[3]

---

[2]The precise location of his birth is not clear. Different sources mention Glen Urquhart, Inchlaggan or Achnaheaglais all of which are, however, clustered close together. See W.J. Macdonell, Reminiscences of the Late Honourable and Right Reverend Alexander Macdonell, (Toronto, 1888), p. 5; J.A. Macdonell, Bishop Macdonell, (Alexandria, 1890), p. 3; Perkins Bull, From Macdonell to McGuigan, (Toronto, 1937), p. 370, n. 5.

[3]The Catholic clans were not, of course, the only ones to support the Jacobite cause, but their identification with the Stuart House drew upon them the heaviest penalties when combined with the penal laws against Roman Catholics.

The wave of repression which swept the Highlands in the wake of the
English victory receded only slowly. There is no evidence, however,
that it left a permanent legacy of bitterness or resentment among the
Macdonells. They were quick to enter military service with the British
when the opportunity arose. Indeed, the future Bishop, who grew up amid
tales of the Highland wars, seemed more British than the English.

There are at least two plausible explanations for this transference
of loyalty. It may be that the Catholics simply resigned themselves to
the inevitable. Abandoned by Prince Charles Stuart, their leadership
decimated, the Highlands ravaged by the army of "German Geordie", the
Macdonells and the other Catholic Clans wished to forget the despair and
horror which followed Culloden. They accepted the military decision,
and managed as best they could in their new circumstances. More subtly,
but not unconnected, the Catholic clergy were coming to positions of
much greater influence as the clan system broke down.[4] It was natural
enough for them to attempt to harmonize the tight hierarchical structure
of the clan and the social implications of eighteenth century Catholicism
with the reality of British power. They could best protect their people,
the clergy reasoned, by inculcating in them the attributes of loyalty
and submissiveness to British authority. In this manner, it was hoped,
some measure of security and competence could be acquired, and their
people held in the Catholic faith. An attendant necessity would be the
continuous recruitment of native clergy.[5] One of these young men

---

[4]See infra, p. 5.

[5]W.F. Leith, Memoirs of Scottish Catholics During the XVIIth and
XVIIIth Centuries, 2 vols., (London, 1909), II, pp. 332-34.

destined for the service of the Church was Alexander Macdonell of

Glengarry.

Macdonell received his early education near his home.[6] Very

likely it was only the most rudimentary instruction, since Catholic

schools were still proscribed by the penal laws. Although their applica-

tion was much relaxed by the early 1770s, there was still considerable

danger as the Gordon riots of 1780, and their repercussions in Scotland,

attested. Just as did other Catholics in the British Isles, it was

necessary for Macdonell to go abroad for his formal religious training.

He was sent to the Scots' College in Paris in 1778 at the age of sixteen

years. From there he went to the Scots' College at Valladolid, Spain.

Generally, the seminary was influenced by post-Suarez theology and morality,

that is, extremely orthodox and conservative. The tendency, then, would

be to deepen and confirm his opinions.[7] Upon completion of his studies

he was ordained February 16, 1787, and returned to the Highlands as a

missionary in August of that year.[8]

---

[6]E. Kelly, The Story of St. Paul's Parish, Toronto, (Toronto, 1922), p. 32; H.J. Somers, The Life and Times of the Honourable and Right Reverend Alexander Macdonell, D.D., (Washington, 1931), p. 9.

[7]Leith, op. cit., II, p. 347.

[8]The information which follows, except where noted, on Macdonell's years from 1787 to 1804 when he emigrated to Upper Canada, is largely drawn from his own account: A Page From the History of the Glengarry Highlanders. There are several variations of this document. It was published over Macdonell's signature in the Canadian Literary Magazine, April, 1833. There are lengthier versions in the Macdonell Papers, in the Archives of the Archdiocese of Kingston (AAK), and in the Macdonell Papers, Public Archives of Canada (PAC), M.G. 24, J13. Various secondary sources have published excerpts from it, but these have been taken from that published in 1833. I have relied on the copy in Macdonell's Papers in the Arch-diocese of Kingston. It is, of course, a biased source, and the tone is somewhat pompous and self-justifying. It appears to be factually correct, however.

For five years, the young priest served in Badenoch, the highest inhabited area of the Highlands. Here, Macdonell and his people were insulated for a time from the traumatic changes which were rupturing the old Highland life. They lived their simple crofter's existence on the edge of subsistence, spoke only Gaelic, and were little aware of the upheaval that would soon affect them. As Macdonell was to recall years later, "The bleak and barren mountains of the north which had previously raised MEN were converted into sheep-walks for the accommodation of a South-Country shepherd". As the demand for pasture land increased, the clan chieftains succumbed to the prospect of higher rents than their tenants could afford. The clan system which had been founded on the reciprocal interests of chief and tenant, collapsed completely.[9] In their bewilderment, as the evictions went on, the people turned to their priests for direction.

Alexander Macdonell's response was to journey to Glasgow to seek employment for his people in the expanding cotton manufacturing concerns located there. Several potential employers offered him encouragement, but warned of the dangers to Catholics because of the penal laws. They were particularly apprehensive when Macdonell expressed his intention of accompanying his people as priest and interpreter, insisting that they had no means of affording protection to a Popish priest. But he would not be dissuaded. Accordingly, in June 1792, he returned to Glasgow and soon found employment for upwards of six hundred of his Highlanders.

---

[9] See H.I. Adam, "The Causes of the Highland Emigrations of 1783-1803", The Scottish Historical Review, 1919-1920, pp. 77-78.

The anticipated difficulties never occurred and the little community
lived in peace and relative prosperity. Even their religious observances
were uninterrupted, as Macdonell recalled complacently:

> But the missionary, by the advice of one of the most
> influential clergymen (Presbyterian) of the city, opened
> his chapel to the street, and did not close the door
> during the service. Two respectable members of the
> Congregation attended, to show any devout persons, at-
> tracted thither by curiosity, into a seat; and several
> who thus came were repeatedly heard to say that this was
> not proper popery at all, although the principal tenets
> of the Catholic religion were taught and explained both
> in English and Gaelic; and because they saw neither
> pictures nor images, and Mass was said very early in
> the morning before those who might be disposed to give
> annoyance were up; and who, being of the lower class of
> laborers and tradesmen, generally spent the Saturday
> evening in a tavern, and the Sunday mornings in bed.

Their new-found comfort was not to last, however. The French
Revolution and the Anglo-French war which broke out in 1793, disrupted
the cotton industry, and provoked heavy unemployment. Once again,
Macdonell's Highlanders were in distress. While he felt his responsibility to his flock acutely, Macdonell also sensed in this misfortune an
opportunity to improve the image of Catholics generally, and Highland
Catholics in particular. There was also the potential advantage of establishing his personal reputation for zealous loyalty, and thus earning favor
with the Ministry. This would strengthen his advocacy considerably.

Macdonell's scheme was to offer the services of his unemployed
people to the government, and have them embodied as a Catholic Corps.
Their commander was to be their young chief, Macdonell of Glengarry. It
was a daring manoeuvre since there had been no Catholic troops as such in
English service for over two centuries. The usual loyal address to the
King was drawn up, and the offer extended. Macdonell led the delegation

to London to present the petition to the government. A fortuitous circumstance forwarded his plan. Several of the Fencible Corps which were raised in Scotland had refused to serve outside the borders of their country.[10] Macdonell's offer became more attractive when he indicated that his Highlanders would serve anywhere in the British Empire that the King's service should require.

The Secretary of State for War, Henry Dundas, welcomed not only the additional manpower, but the creation of a precedent which would permit deployment of the Fencible Corps wherever they were needed. The necessary commissions were struck embodying the First Glengarry Fencible Corps for service anywhere in Great Britain and Ireland, and the islands of Jersey and Guernsey. It was the first Catholic regiment to be raised in Britain since the Reformation, and Macdonell took intense pride in the fact that he was officially gazetted as chaplain.[11]

In the summer of 1795, the regiment was ordered to Guernsey which was thought to be threatened with invasion from the French coast. There it remained, in relative inactivity, until rebellion broke out in Ireland in 1798. Macdonell's regiment was then transferred to duty in County Wexford, the seat of the Rising. They served there throughout the disturbances. Macdonell suggested in his long memoir that because of his

---

[10]They apparently took the designation Fencible literally. Military histories are somewhat contradictory on this point, but apparently Fencible Corps were considered equivalent to a home defense force. See Sir J.W. Fortescue, History of the British Army, 13 vols., (London, 1915), vol. 4, part 2, pp. 889-91; App. E, p. 943.

[11]There is a copy of his commission, signed by George III, among Macdonell's papers in the Archdiocesan Archives of Kingston. It should be noted, however, that there were Catholic troops in the service of James II in 1688-89.

influence over the Highlanders their conduct and discipline appeared exem-
plary in contrast to the activities of other British troops in Ireland.
This not only enhanced their reputation with the British Government, but
allowed them to make contact with their Irish co-religionists. They
induced many of them to return to more peaceful ways by pointing to the
treatment Scots Catholics had earned by their loyalty. Macdonell claimed
as well that he acted as liaison between the leaders of Irish Catholics
and the British Government on the question of the legislative union of
Ireland and Great Britain which was completed in 1800. The British
authorities were informed by Macdonell that the Catholic Bishops and
leading Catholic laymen would lend their support to the proposal. Lord
Castlereagh, Chief Secretary for Ireland, fowarded conflicting information.
As Macdonell wrote later:

> This the Chaplain [Macdonell] took the liberty to deny, and
> offered to prove his assertion to the satisfaction of
> Mr. Dundas by being allowed time to refer to the Catholic
> meeting at Dublin. He accordingly wrote to Colonel Macdonell,
> whom he had left in that city, and received by return of post,
> an answer from Viscount Kenmare, contradicting in toto the
> assertions of Viscount Castlereagh. On this occasion the
> Government papers indulged in severe reflections upon the
> conduct of the Irish Catholics. The Chaplain requested that
> they should be contradicted, which was done very reluctantly
> and not until he threatened to have the truth published in
> the Opposition papers. The correspondence on that subject
> is now in his possession.[12]

This incident has been recorded to illustrate two facets of
Macdonell's attitudes at this stage of his career. He was convinced
that the status of Catholics under British rule was inextricably bound

---

[12]A search of Macdonell's papers has failed to turn up this
correspondence.

up with their reputation for loyalty; and no opportunity should be lost to make this manifest. Any assumption that Catholics, even Irish Catholics, were anti-British must be contested.[13] This did not, however, mean servility, and Macdonell never avoided controversy in his attempts to make his point that religious loyalty to hierarchically-structured Catholicism would strengthen political loyalty to hierarchically-structured Britain. At the same time, he wished to make himself as useful as possible to the British Government, and broaden his network of connections with people in positions of power. In this way, he hoped to be of greater service in forwarding the interests of his people. Macdonell frankly accepted, and never seems to have questioned, the degree to which influence and patronage were determining factors in the advancement of persons and projects.

He returned to Ireland and remained there with his regiment until 1802 when the Fencibles were disbanded during the brief Peace of Amiens. Upon learning that there was little hope of finding employment again in Scottish industry, Macdonell hoped that his claim upon the government was now sufficiently well established that he could secure grants of land for the Highlanders in Upper Canada. His selection of the newly-created province as a refuge was due largely to the fact that those Glengarry people who had emigrated to America much earlier, and fought as Loyalists in the American Revolution under Sir John Johnson, were already settled in the eastern region of Upper Canada. He had only the vaguest knowledge

---

[13] It should be noted that Macdonell at this time was dealing with the Irish Catholic gentry. The mass of Irish Catholics would present severe problems for him later in Upper Canada, yet his general opinion on this question did not change.

of conditions in the new province; but expected to find it similar to the Highlands and thus a familiar environment for his flock.

III

Accordingly, Macdonell set out from Ireland for London to present his project to the British Government, relying heavily on the fact that the services of the regiment and his own personal credit would merit a favourable reception. Henry Addington,[14] who had briefly succeeded William Pitt as Prime Minister, proved to be favourably disposed. While he expressed regret that conditions in Scotland made it necessary for the Highlanders to emigrate, he seemed willing to aid Macdonell's plan. As the latter recorded the negotiations in his memoir, however, Addington appeared intent on directing the emigration of the Highlanders to the political advantage of Britain. To better establish imperial control of the island of Trinidad, which had been ceded to Britain by the Treaty of Amiens, the Prime Minister encouraged Macdonell to lead his people to the West Indies. An inducement was proposed of lands, slaves and partial maintenance for three years for every settler introduced. Macdonell demurred on the ground that he could not take responsibility for advising his adherents to locate in such an unhealthy climate and maintained his preference for Upper Canada.

---

[14]Addington was raised to the peerage in 1805 as Lord Sidmouth. In 1812 he became Home Secretary in the Liverpool Government and served for ten years. He died in 1844. Macdonell corresponded with him over the years; and despite Sidmouth's rather narrow views, and his reputation as a high churchman, he gave what assistance he could to Macdonell in Upper Canada.

Addington's reluctance to endorse the Canadian venture was founded on his belief that Britain's hold on Upper Canada was "so slender and so precarious that a person in his situation would not be justified in putting his hand in the public purse to assist British subjects to emigrate to that colony". This argument Macdonell quickly turned to his own advantage. It was precisely because the Highlanders had so clearly demonstrated their valour and loyalty in the field that they would be best fitted to secure the province for the King. He suggested to Addington that the Highlanders be sent out as military units to accomplish the dual purpose of settlement and protection, thus strengthening the connection with the mother country. After a short period of service the men would be granted land on generous terms. "It would settle the country with loyal and respectable inhabitants who, by having a stake in the country, would feel zeal and interest in the defence of it." Macdonell indicated in his recollections that the Prime Minister was about to approve this scheme when the war with France resumed, and Addington gave way to Pitt. In Upper Canada, Macdonell maintained his interest in compact military settlement, and on several occasions used his influence to support such experiments.

Before he left office, however, Addington secured the King's authorization for a grant of two hundred acres of land in Upper Canada for every soldier of the Glengarry Regiment that Macdonell should induce to emigrate.[15] Considerable pressure was brought to bear on Macdonell

---

[15]P.A.C., C042, vol. 331, Lord Hobart, Colonial Secretary to Lieutenant General Hunter, Lieutenant Governor of Upper Canada, 1 March 1803.

by the Highland proprietors in an attempt to dissuade him from leading a large emigration. They feared a mass exodus of their tenants. According to Macdonell, this fear resulted in the passage of a new, more stringent Passenger Act which so regulated conditions aboard the emigrant ships that few of the poor Highlanders would be able to defray the increased costs of passage.[16] Lord Hobart, the Colonial Secretary, in an effort to ease the blow, urged Macdonell to take his people by way of New York. Thus they would enter Upper Canada from the United States and qualify for an additional two hundred acres per man under the terms of Lieutenant Governor Simcoe's proclamation of 1792.[17]

> This Mr. McDonell[18] peremptorily refused to do, for two reasons, first because it was a more circuitous and consequently a more expensive route, and secondly he did not wish his adherents to be innoculated with republican principles . . . which they could hardly avoid imbibing in travelling through the United States.

Now impatient to be going, the Highlanders made their own way to Upper Canada, relying on the promise of grants of land and the expected welcome among their friends and kinsmen already settled in the eastern end of

---

[16] George III cap. 56. Statutes United Kingdom, 41 to 43 George III, Vol. 1. This legislation has normally been interpreted as humanitarian in intent; but Macdonell's argument is at least plausible since the Highland landowners gave vigorous support, government ships were excluded from provisions of the legislation, and it was amended the following year (44 George III cap. 54) to exclude the Newfoundland trade. See also James Brown, The History of Scotland, 8 vols., Vol. 8, pp. 146-47.

[17] E.A. Cruikshank, ed., The Correspondence of Lieut. Governor John Graves Simcoe, 5 vols., (Toronto, 1923-31), I, p. 108-09.

[18] Until 1838, when he was 76 years of age, the Bishop consistently spelled his name in this manner. At that time he abruptly switched to Macdonell. Since the latter spelling is the more familiar since his death, I have employed it, except in direct quotation.

Upper Canada. The government, meanwhile, had made one final overture to
Macdonell to alter his plans. Charles Phillip Yorke, Secretary at War
in the Addington Ministry, appealed directly to his sense of loyalty,
and tried to persuade Macdonell to bring his men back into the army in
view of the threatening situation on the continent.[19] But it was now
too late.

Macdonell remained behind briefly to settle his personal affairs.
He was contacted by the Earl of Selkirk who attempted to entice him to
join an emigration scheme which Selkirk proposed to locate in the region
"between Lakes Huron and Superior". Indeed, Macdonell claimed that Selkirk
offered him a personal inducement of ₤2000 if he would lend his support
to the project. The priest refused, however, on the grounds that the
area was too remote, that it was beyond the jurisdiction of the government
of Upper Canada, and that

> . . . such a settlement would entirely destroy the North-
> West Company, as it would cut off the communications
> between the winterers and Canada; and as several of the
> principal members of that company were his particular
> friends, no consideration would induce him to enter
> upon an enterprise that would injure their interest.[20]

Macdonell then concluded his business and took ship for Canada in the
summer of 1804.

---

[19] AAK, Macdonell Papers, Yorke to Macdonell, 7 June, 26 August, 1803.

[20] PAC, MG 24, J 13, Macdonell Papers. The Selkirk incident is
described at greatest length in the version of Macdonell's memoir in the
Ottawa Archives. The reference to the North-West Company pertains
especially to the McGillivray family with whom Macdonell had close
connections in Canada in his later years.

There is no telling, of course, what preoccupied Macdonell's mind during the tedious Atlantic passage. But some apprehension on his part would not be unjustified. He had directed those who relied upon him to a colony which had been organized only a dozen years. Very little of it had as yet been redeemed from the wilderness. The Church of England, if not uncontestedly the established church, was secure in its preferred position. He himself would be subject to the ecclesiastical authority of the French Canadian Bishop.

But he could take some comfort in the hope that his people could hardly be worse off than facing the bleak future of the depressed Highlands. They had the King's promise of land. There was the prospect of their own community sheltered by the Gaelic and the faith. And through his own agency, they would not be without friends. The military commanders under whom they had served would willingly provide testimony to their loyalty and good conduct. In the remote area of the British Empire that was Upper Canada one such person was already in a position to lend them aid. Lieutenant Governor Peter Hunter had replied to the Colonial Secretary that he should

> . . . have much pleasure in paying every attention to
> Mr. Macdonell, upon his arrival in this country . . . and
> should [be] very glad to [see] the disbanded soldiers of
> the Glengarry Fencible Regiment settled in Upper Canada.
> That Regiment served some short time under my command in
> Ireland in 1798, when I found them to be a remarkably
> well behaved and well disposed set of people.[21]

---

[21] PAC, CO42, vol. 336, Hunter to Hobart, 20 June, 1804.

There was also the satisfaction of knowing that they would be settling in a British colony. The efforts of the preceding ten years and the connections established could be built upon profitably. The willing submission of the Highlanders to his leadership would ensure their continuance in the faith, their allegiance to the British crown, and their insulation from "republican principles". To Alexander Macdonell it was a broad enough perch from which he and his people could approach their adventure in Upper Canada.

CHAPTER II

SINKING ROOTS

I

It seemed clear to Macdonell, in view of his experience, that the success of the new venture would depend to a great extent on the ability of himself and his people to secure and maintain the beneficent interest of the provincial authorities. The letters of introduction which he carried, and the reputation which the Highlanders had earned during the war, were an adequate beginning. But Macdonell realized that past services alone would not guarantee the continuing support of government. Upper Canada was far removed from the centre of British power where, due largely to his own efforts, his flock was held in some esteem. The local government of Upper Canada must also be made aware of the potential usefulness of compact settlements of loyal Scottish Catholics.

At the same time, Macdonell's capacity to forward the interests of his people and his religion would increase markedly if he were able to ingratiate himself with the government at York. As he interpreted the political and social complexion of the province in his early years there, this could be best accomplished through personal contact, effective political support of the provincial government, and shrewd exploitation of the mixed character of the province's population. By juxtaposing the established loyal tradition of his Highlanders over against the potentially

16

volatile, if not dangerous, growing American element in Upper Canada, Macdonell hoped that the government would draw the anticipated conclusion. Social and political stability would be best secured by open encouragement shown to the dependable portion of His Majesty's subjects. The public manifestation of this support would take the form of land grants and advancement in the patronage system for Scots Catholics. He hoped, as well, that it would be recognized that a major buttress of Upper Canada could be found in the social implications of Catholicism as represented by himself.

To give effect to this intention, he frequently employed the danger of American ideological penetration of the province as a foil. The alarm raised by the Chesapeake affair in 1807 added a physical threat which Macdonell used to add weight to his contentions. When war did break out in 1812, the alacrity with which the Highlanders of the Eastern District of the province responded was a capstone to his persistent campaign, and seemed to justify the career he had pursued from the time of his arrival in the province.

II

Upon his arrival in British North America, in the autumn of 1804, Father Macdonell first contacted his prospective religious superior, Bishop J.O. Plessis, in Montreal.[1] It marked the beginning of a long

---

[1] Rapport de l'Archiviste de la Province de Quebec (R.A.Q.), 1927-28; Correspondence of Bishop Plessis, p. 236; Plessis to Bishop Denault, Quebec, 15 October 1804, announcing the arrival of Macdonell. Plessis was then co-adjutor to Bishop Denault, and would succeed him as Bishop of Quebec two years later.

and mutually advantageous relationship between the two men. Indeed,
Plessis was almost the only member of the Quebec hierarchy in whom
Macdonell had much confidence over the years. Macdonell then proceeded
to Longueuil to meet Bishop Denault, who was visiting in that area, and
receive from him the necessary ecclesiastical authorization to assume
his ministry in Upper Canada which was then under the jurisdiction of
the Bishop of Quebec.[2]

Macdonell was equally anxious to see to the temporal affairs of
his flock; so he went immediately to York to greet General Hunter and
secure the land grants which had been promised before the departure from
Great Britain. Meeting with initial success, although it would take
some time for the actual title deeds to be issued, Macdonell remained in
York briefly, hoping to win Hunter's support for a broad programme of
assisted emigration from the Highlands. The attraction for these potential settlers would be not only the abundant land available in Upper
Canada; but

> . . . other inducements that would undoubtedly prove still
> more powerful in determining their choice in favour of this
> province, and those are affording them the means of exercising
> their religion and educating their children. Such measures
> at the same time that they would be attended with the most
> salutary and beneficial effects to the people, could not fail
> of producing consequences of the first importance to the State.
> Your Excellency must be aware that the strongest pledge which
> the Mother Country can hold of the loyalty and attachment of
> Scots Highlanders to their Sovereign, and to the British
> constitution is by preserving their national characteristics,
> by keeping them as much as possible seperate [sic] and distinct

---

[2]Ibid., p. 80, Denault to Hunter, 22 October 1804. Denault accords
Macdonell a rather glowing introduction, and hints that the newly-arrived
priest should be eligible for a government salary.

from other classes of people in this Country, and by fostering,
and fomenting their virtuous and loyal principles with the
instructions, and exhortations of their countrymen in their
native language.[3]

This was the opening shot in a long, and eventually successful
campaign by Macdonell to win government support for Catholic clergy and
teachers. It would, he was convinced, serve several purposes. By making
priests and teachers dependent on the state, their attachment would be
direct and personal; and their steady loyalty thus assured. It would as
well, impose an obligation on the government for the continuing support
of Catholicism; a situation eminently desirable in Macdonell's view since
it would mean official recognition and a secure future for the faith.
Furthermore, the influence of these community leaders over the people,
Macdonell reasoned, would be greatly increased if priests were not
obliged to rely completely upon their congregations for their maintenance.
He would return again and again to these themes in his struggle to gain
financial assistance from the government. For the moment, he was content
to bring to Hunter's attention the desirability of increased Highland
settlement.

After this first journey to York--no light undertaking in those
days of difficult, if not hazardous travel Macdonell returned to Glengarry
to take up his duties as missionary to the Catholics of the Eastern
District. He busied himself organizing his charge, acting as liaison
with the government for land deeds for the immigrants and planning the

---

[3] A.A.K., Macdonell Papers, Macdonell to Hunter, 11 November
1804.

erection of a new church. He had been assured his own salary would come
from Quebec. Indeed, it had already been authorized by Governor-in-Chief
Robert Milne.[4] As months passed and he heard nothing further, he decided
to proceed to Montreal. Once there he sought the intercession of Joseph
Frobisher, one of the original founders of the North West Company and,
until his retirement, a senior partner in the powerful firm of McTavish,
Frobisher and Co. Frobisher responded with a letter to the government
and the delay ended. Macdonell's salary of £50 annually continued
regularly until it was increased a few years later.[5]

While he was in Montreal, an interview with Plessis resulted in
the extension of Macdonell's responsibility. He was informed that he
would shortly be named Vicar General of Upper Canada. The Bishop also
charged Macdonell to petition for and receive lands for church sites in
Kingston and York. Plessis thus hoped to inflate Macdonell's standing
with the local government, since the Bishop was already planning the
division of the diocese of Quebec which, in fact, included all of British
North America at this time. In addition, Plessis agreed to help bear the
expense of educating children for the priesthood when Macdonell sent them
to the seminaries of Montreal and Quebec.[6]

Upon his return to Glengarry, Macdonell set about establishing
himself within the political system of the province. Alexander Grant
had just been appointed President and Administrator of Upper Canada upon

---

[4]Report of the Public Archives of Canada, 1896, p. 80, Milne to
Robert Coldwell, Receiver General, 31 July 1805.

[5]Ibid., p. 81, Frobisher to Green, 3 February 1806.

[6]R.A.Q., Plessis Correspondence, pp. 240-41; Plessis to Macdonell
7 February 1806.

the death of General Hunter. He had also come from Inverness-shire, and
Macdonell found in him a sympathetic and effective advocate. Through
Grant, he was able to make a beginning in having members of his flock
appointed to government service. After successfully securing the appointment of a surveyor for the Eastern District,[7] he reminded the Administrator
that

> I had the honor to speak to you when at York on the
> subject of appointing a sheriff to this District when
> your honor was so very kind as to say that you would
> pay attention to my recommendation to that appointment.

Macdonell went on to recommend his cousin, Miles Macdonell, later
Governor of Assiniboia, for the vacant office.[8]

He was also anxious to use Grant's good offices to have more land
set aside for church and settlement purposes as Plessis had urged. In
a petition to the President, Macdonell played on Grant's affection for
the Scots, and justified his request with the argument

> . . . that so respectable a population would prove a
> strong barrier against the contagion of Republican
> principles so rapidly diffusing among the people of
> this Province by the industry of the settlers from the
> United States, and would prevent any general combination
> that could be formed against the Government.[9]

---

[7] P.A.C., Upper Canada Sundries, Macdonell to Grant, 17 March 1806.

[8] Ibid., Macdonell to Grant, 11 June 1806. Macdonell did not press
the recommendation of his cousin at that time. The priest was annoyed
that Miles was, at the time, negotiating to enter the service of Lord
Selkirk; and he feared Selkirk's plans would pose a threat to the North
West Company. See also, A.G. Morice, "Sidelights on the Careers of Miles
Macdonell and his Brothers", Canadian Historical Review, (C.H.R.),
December 1929, passim.

[9] P.A.C., C042, vol. 342, Grant to Castlereagh, 5 May 1806;
Macdonell's petition enclosed.

Grant apparently agreed; and he forwarded the petition to Lord Castlereagh, then Secretary of State for War and the Colonies, with his approval, adding that, "The character and conduct of Mr. Macdonell are such as to entitle him to the indulgence of Government".[10] That same summer of 1806, Macdonell was invited to the general examinations of the school conducted by John Strachan at Cornwall in the Eastern District.[11] The two men may have met previously, but this is the first evidence of a public relationship between the two who, along with Egerton Ryerson, would dominate the religious life of Upper Canada until 1840 and beyond.

Indicative of the manner in which politics and patronage were conducted in early Upper Canada was Macdonell's sense of urgency in establishing relations with Francis Gore, the new Lieutenant Governor of the Province. His personal connection with Grant had proven very useful, but he was essentially in locum tenens. From Macdonell's point of view, much would depend on obtaining a similar rapport with the official representative of the Crown.

The first step was a formal introduction by his religious superior;[12] and then his position was enhanced shortly after, when Bishop Plessis informed Gore that he had named Macdonell, Vicar General of Upper Canada. In his announcement to the Lieutenant Governor, Plessis

---

[10] Ibid.

[11] Upper Canada Gazette, 24 August 1806.

[12] R.A.Q., Plessis Correspondence, Plessis to Gore, 25 August 1806.

emphasized the benefits of that necessary connection between church and state which, of course, Macdonell exemplified.[13] The latter, meanwhile, had been utilizing his acquaintance with Thomas Scott, formerly the Attorney General who was named Chief Justice of Upper Canada in 1806. Scott used his considerable influence in aiding Macdonell's plan to acquire land throughout the province for future locations of churches and schools.[14]

It was Bishop Plessis' intention to move as quickly as possible in the matter of the division of his immense diocese. He recognized that it would be an extremely delicate business. The legal position of the Roman Catholic Church in British North America was still somewhat anomalous because it was denied recognition by the laws of England. By forcing the question of the creation of new sees under the auspices of the government, at least tacit, if not outright recognition of the Church would have to be accorded. In the event, it took Plessis ten years to accomplish his objective, and Alexander Macdonell was to play a key role in its fulfillment. As early as March 1807, in a letter which Macdonell presented to Gore, Plessis indicated that he had charged the bearer with "une mission tróc importante pour les Catholiques due Canada".[15] The Bishop informed Macdonell that he hoped to nominate him bishop in partibus with jurisdiction over all of Upper Canada. But it must be accomplished

---

[13] Ibid., Plessis to Gore, 14 March 1807. See also Bull, From Macdonell to MacGuigan, p. 101.

[14] P.A.C., Upper Canada Sundries, Scott to William Halton (Secretary to Gore), 17 September 1806; in which he supports Macdonell's application for a lot in Trafalgar Township.

[15] R.A.Q., Plessis Correspondence, Plessis to Gore, 14 March 1807.

with the consent and approbation of the government. Macdonell, thus, was instructed by Plessis, to impress upon Gore 'malgré tous les obstacles qui peuvent s'opposer à sa réalisation . . . tous les avantages qui résulteront de la nomination d'un évêque catholique dans le Haut-Canada".[16] Macdonell, of course, pointed out to the Bishop that Gore could make no such decision; but Plessis urged him to attempt to persuade Gore to lend his support to the project.[17]

The martial reputation of the Highlanders was also turned to account as Macdonell suggested to Gore, Isaac Brock, Sir James Craig, and anyone else who would listen, that the men of Glengarry should be incorporated as a militia regiment. He pointed out the obvious advantages to the government in view of the deteriorating relations between Britain and the United States. There were other potential benefits as well. His constant extolling of the loyalty of Scots Catholics would be made manifest; and many of them would be recognized by the government with commissions. Craig, the Governor-in-Chief, was sufficiently impressed to give his official sanction, and Brock was enthusiastic. The latter wrote to the Secretary for War, recommending acceptance of the offer, and remarked,

> In regard to the Reverend Alexander Macdonell I beg leave
> to observe that the men, being all Catholics, it may be
> deemed a prudent measure to appoint him Chaplain. His
> zeal and attachment to Government were strongly evinced
> while filling the office of Chaplain to the Glengarry

---

[16]Ibid., Plessis to Macdonell, 15 March 1807.

[17]Ibid., Plessis to Macdonell, 23 April 1807.

Fencibles during the rebellion in Ireland, and were
graciously acknowledged by His Royal Highness the
Commander-in-Chief.

His influence over the men is deservedly great, and I
have every reason to believe that the Corps, by his
exertions, would be soon completed, and hereafter become
a nursery, from which the army might draw a number of
hardy recruits.[18]

This, of course, was precisely the kind of reaction for which Macdonell

hoped; and his connection with Brock would very soon prove valuable.

Gore, as well, was sympathetic, and he informed Craig that he had "every

reason to believe that it is only by the Agency of their own Countrymen

that those people would be induced to inlist [sic]".[19]

Macdonell was quick to take advantage of his growing contact with

the Lieutenant Governor to urge his favourite scheme.

I am every day more and more convinced that it would be a
measure of no less importance to the Government than to
the Scots Catholics of this Province themselves to have
their clergymen selected from their own countrymen and
educated either in Britain or in this same Province, who
should rest their principle [sic] dependence on the
Government itself.[20]

In his attempt to win Gore's favour, he could be almost sycophantic, as

in his endeavour to capitalize on the excitement created by the

Chesapeake affair, when he wrote that

. . . it is with the greatest pleasure that I have to
inform his Excellency that all the Highlanders of these
settlements express an ardent desire of seconding any

---

[18]Cited in J.A. Macdonell, op. cit., pp. 126-27; see also Lucas,
War of 1812, (Oxford, 1906), p. 13.

[19]P.A.C., Upper Canada Sundries, Gore to Craig, 4 April 1808.

[20]Ibid., Macdonell to Gore, 21 January 1808.

measure he may adopt for the security of the Country
and support of the Government.[21]

In a public address designed to encourage support for the Lieutenant

Governor and his administration, Macdonell's name was in a prominent

position.[22]

While he was thus engaged in cultivating the leading men in British

North America, Macdonell was distracted by a family difficulty that was

intruding on another of his interests. His cousin Miles had by now

determined to join Lord Selkirk's proposed settlement in the Northwest,

much to the priest's chagrin. In a long letter to John Macdonell,

brother of Miles and a wintering partner of the North West Company,

Father Macdonell opined that he began

> . . . to entertain strong apprehensions that [Miles] will
> find himself much disappointed in the sanguine hopes placed
> in his Lordship, and that it would have been more to his
> interest and to his credit to have remained at home in
> Scothouse and mind his own affairs than [to] dance
> attendance to the Earl of Selkirk . . . entering contrary
> to his own judgement and good sense into the fantastical
> scheme of his Lordship.[23]

His opinion of Selkirk was dictated by his close associations with the

principal figures in the North West Company. He depended upon them for

assistance both financial and otherwise; as he indicated to John;

> Mr. McGilivray's [sic] conduct . . . has always been like
> that of a brother, and indeed I must acknowledge that I
> have not a friend or relative in the world for whom I have
> a warmer regard and higher esteem. I expect to get the

---

[21] Ibid., Macdonell to Halton, 31 January 1808.

[22] Upper Canada Gazette, 9 June 1810.

[23] A.G. Morice, op. cit., p. 314, citing Alexander Macdonell to
John Macdonell, 14 June 1811.

> Church at Kingston entirely finished this year, and I
> intend to allot a pew in front of the gallery for the use
> of the N.W. Co., to show my grateful sense of their
> liberal donation towards building it.[24]

It was with considerable skepticism, then, that the priest referred to

a letter which Miles had written to Strachan in which his cousin

disclaimed any intention of becoming involved in a scheme which might

jeopardize the interests of the Northwesters.[25] But his preoccupation

with these matters quickly dissipated when Upper Canada was thrown into

alarm at the threatening situation developing in the affairs of Britain

and the United States.

For Macdonell, given his opinion of American republicanism, the

response would be automatic. With his characteristic energy and eye to

advantage, he threw himself into the preparations for war which were

going forward in the province. His reputation, and that of the High-

landers, would be put to the test. But any hazard would be outweighed

by the opportunity offered by the emergency to gain the recognition

and approbation of the government.

III

As early as 1807 Macdonell had begun advocating the embodiment

of a militia corps in Glengarry, and had won the support of Isaac Brock

and Governor Craig. This initial attempt had not been successful due

---

[24]Ibid.

[25]Ibid. This suggests that Macdonell and Strachan must have been
on quite intimate terms at this date.

to the lukewarm response of the British Government.[26] But the complexion

of the situation had altered markedly; and the new Governor General and

Commander of the Forces, Sir George Prevost, gave his warm encouragement

to the project soon after he took office. Macdonell received the

information from Plessis, who informed him that "le capitaine Miles

Macdonell . . . s'en va lever un corps de militaires dans le district

de Glengarry".[27] The Bishop had made a not uncommon error in confusing

the many Macdonells. He was referring to Captain George Macdonell,

better known among his compatriots as "Red George". Miles was on his

way to Red River at this time, in the employ of Lord Selkirk.

Father Macdonell immediately accompanied Captain George Macdonell

to York to consult Brock, who was now Commander of the Forces in Upper

Canada. Again, the General endorsed the raising of a regiment of High-

landers in Glengarry. It was not simply because he welcomed the additional

manpower. His estimate of the loyalty of some elements of the population

in Upper Canada, and of the French-Canadians, was sharply unflattering.

He considered it a distinct advantage to have a proven regiment in the

Eastern District on the border of Lower Canada.[28] During their discussions,

Brock was persuaded by Father Macdonell to hasten enlistments by the pro-

mise of land grants. In his civil capacity of President and Administrator,

---

[26]
  W. Wood, Select British Documents of the War of 1812, (Toronto,
1920), Vol. I, pp. 297-98. Liverpool to Prevost, 12 March 1812.

[27] R.A.Q., Plessis Correspondence, Plessis to Macdonell, 9 December
1811.

[28] J.A. Macdonell, op. cit., p. 29; Lucas, op. cit., p. 13.

Brock, of course, had such authority; and the advantage to the men of Glengarry would be obvious.

The most important strategic difficulty with which Brock was faced was the maintenance of his line of communication with the lower province. The St. Lawrence water route would be open to constant harassment from the American shore. What was vitally necessary, Brock concluded, was an adequate road link between the provinces which could be more easily defended. Macdonell's carefully cultivated reputation in the Eastern District, through which such a road must pass, and his thorough knowledge of it, led Brock to take advantage of his services. He instructed the priest to return eastward to meet Prevost, and in his report he explained to the Governor-in-Chief that, "the Reverend Mr. Macdonell of Glengarry, the bearer of this letter, is so well qualified to explain the causes which have hitherto impeded the cutting of a road to connect the two Provinces that I need not detain Your Excellency".[29] Macdonell was able to act as liaison on the road project, and he was rewarded the following year by his first major appointment from the government. He was named Commissioner to undertake construction of the road with authority to oversee the expenditure of government funds; and it was Brock's desire that Macdonell "be consulted in all matters concerning it".[30]

Not only did this direct recognition by the government add to

---

[29]Cited in J.A. Macdonell, op. cit., pp. 31-32, Brock to Prevost, 26 January 1812.

[30]P.A.C., RG 8, Series C, vol. 688a, 12 June 1813, pp. 58-59.

Macdonell's prestige, it allowed him to advance the interests of his people in Glengarry. Many of them found employment building the road, and he was able to have his young cousin, Allan Macdonell, appointed as one of the other two commissioners.[31] The position was by no means a sinecure, however, and Macdonell was obliged to expend considerable time and energy in its execution. He continued in his capacity as Commissioner until the road was completed in the summer of 1814. It added substantially to his reputation for usefulness to government; and at the same time inflated his position in the Eastern District, due partly to the patronage he was authorized to dispense.[32] It also permitted him, in the course of his duties, to acquire detailed information about the unallocated lands as yet available in the District.

Macdonell was hopeful that they would be filled up by further immigration of Scots Catholics. As was his custom he maintained that the State would be an immediate beneficiary of such a policy. It was in this vein that he cast his proposal to Sir George Murray, who was briefly the provisional Lieutenant Governor of Upper Canada,

> I have the honor to acknowledge receipt of your Excellency's favor of the 30th ulto. I feel great satisfaction to think that your Excellency should concur with me in opinion that Scotch emigrants who may be expected this season ought to be settled in the neighbourhood of their Countrymen already established in this District.

---

[31] P.A.C., Upper Canada Sundries, Macdonell to Loring (secretary), 27 April, 2 May 1814; see also, J.G. Harkness, Stormont, Dundas, and Glengarry, (Oshawa, 1946), p. 127.

[32] P.A.C., Upper Canada Sundries, Macdonell to Loring, 27 April, 2 May 1814.

> The reasons for such an arrangement are too obvious to
> escape the observation of any man possessed of the
> topographical knowledge of this part of the Province,
> and reflects for a moment on the political circumstances
> of the Country.[33]

The influx would also have the effect of putting an end to what Macdonell

saw as an expansionist threat from Lower Canada. As he reported to Murray

> . . . the division line between this and the Lower Province
> has never been yet run, that the adjoining French Seigniors
> taking advantage of this circumstance, sent out Surveyors
> of their own without the knowledge or concurrence of the
> Govert who thought proper to incroach not only upon the
> [lands] above mentioned, but even to annex to the Seignories
> [sic] of their employers several farms belonging to this
> County the proprietors of which altho in possession of
> their farms since the commencement of this settlement,
> and held them upon the same tenure as the rest of the
> inhabitants of the county, were through fear of being
> deprived of the fruit of so many years hard labor induced
> to pay rent to their pretended landlords, till I with the
> sanction of Governor Gore put a stop to them.[34]

The advent of war meant as well the injection of a strident note

into the politics of the province. Isaac Brock's dubious opinion of the

dependability of recently arrived settlers from the United States was

reflected in the government's determination to ensure that the right

sort of people were returned to the Assembly of Upper Canada. Thus the

election of 1812 would involve to a very marked degree what passed at

the time for a loyalty test. In Glengarry, which returned two members

to the House of Assembly, there was no serious apprehension. Traditionally,

---

[33]P.A.C., MG 24, A 11, Sir George Murray Papers, Macdonell to
Murray, 18 May 1815.

[34]Ibid.

the members elected were either Macdonells or men married to Macdonells.[35]
Political activity revolved around the question of whether Catholic or
Presbyterian Scots should have the honour of representing the County.
Both groups, however, were overwhelmingly Tory; and elections there were
essentially faction fights within that body of opinion. The 1812 contest
resulted in the selection of the Attorney General, Col. John Macdonell,
who was subsequently killed with Brock at Queenston Heights; and Alexander
McMartin, a prominent Presbyterian, who held his seat, except for a four
year interval, from 1812-34.

The government was considerably more concerned with the adjoining
County of Stormont. The sitting member, Abraham Marsh, had not been a
warm supporter of the government and there was some anxiety that he might
be re-elected. Father Macdonell, knowing that Glengarry was secure, took
a hand in the Stormont election on behalf of John Beikie, the government
candidate. One of Macdonell's political contacts at York was Archibald
McLean, from Glengarry, who would have a long and distinguished career
as politician and jurist culminating in his appointment as Chief Justice
of the Court of Queen's Bench in 1862. At the time, he was practising
law in York and taking an active interest in the election campaign. He
was relying on Macdonell to swing Stormont into the government column.

---

[35]Harkness, op. cit., pp. 85-92. "This family of Macdonell's
seems to have had a monopoly of Parliamentary honours in the early days
of Glengarry and it is interesting to note that, of the members elected
to the Assembly from 1792 to 1840, all were connected either by blood
or marriage with the Macdonells . . . except Alexander McMartin and
John Cameron."

Mr. Beikie yesterday received a letter from you and is much encouraged by its contents. He goes down, I believe, with the bearer, J. McDonell [Col. John, who would be elected in Glengarry], to propose himself as a candidate. I sincerely hope that neither of them will be disappointed in the object of their journey, as at this time it is particularly to be desired that the House of Assembly should be composed of well-informed men who are well affected to the Government. I hope Mr. Marsh will not be returned again. I was sorry to see him returned at the last Election, as the most fit and discreet Person to represent the County of Stormont. But I hope that the inhabitants will so far retrieve their lost reputation as to send a proper Person to represent them in the next Parliament. If Beikie does not succeed I shall lose my good opinion of the penetration and sense of the County which I should be very sorry to do.[36]

Stormont's reputation in the eyes of McLean was secure, however, as Macdonell's exertions on behalf of Beikie contributed to the result which placed that county in the government camp.[37] Since this was the first election in which Macdonell had attempted to campaign on behalf of the government beyond the boundaries of Glengarry, the outcome must have been gratifying to him. If any justification for his direct intervention were needed--and it would scarcely occur to him-- the outbreak of war the following month would remove all doubts.

His conduct during the course of the war was characterized by an almost extravagant loyalty. Not only had he been instrumental in raising the Glengarry Regiment; he was gazetted as Chaplain and accompanied the men in the field. At the battle of Ogdensburg, he particularly distinguished himself, and earned the thanks of George Macdonell,

---

[36]Archives of the Archdiocese of Toronto (A.A.T.), Macdonell Papers, McLean to Macdonell, 20 May 1812.

[37]Harkness, op. cit., p. 90.

then Lieutenant Colonel, who wrote that

> I have long seen with admiration the zealous measures
> you have invariably pursued, since the commencement of
> hostilities, to stimulate and encourage the valuable
> Highland population of this District under the many
> privations they must unavoidably experience from being
> in the immediate vicinity of the Seat of War--and I am
> convinced that your address to that portion of my embodied
> militia under your pastoral care, on the eve of the
> attack on the 22nd inst. contributed much to the decided
> and persevering gallantry which allowed no obstacle to
> resist them.[38]

Traditional Canadian accounts of the war almost all refer to the part

played by Macdonell. They range from the well-documented history of

Lucas, which praised his contribution, especially that which "has largely

created the new regiment, still serving with them as their chaplain and

guide, and sharing their toils and privations in the field;" to the

romantic memoir of William Coffin, who recalled Macdonell as "Partaking

of the character of the medieval churchman, half bishop, half baron, he

fought and prayed, with equal zeal, by the side of the men he had come

to regard as his hereditary followers".[39] This latter hyperbole might

well have accorded with Macdonell's own interpretation of his wartime

exertions. Certainly, he felt quite justified in exploiting the reputa-

tion for devoted service to the Crown which he was convinced he had

earned.

Even before the war had ended he was making plans to institution-

alize his Catholic conservatism and endeavouring to capitalize on the

---

[38]Cited in Sommers, op. cit., George Macdonell to Alexander Macdonell
28 February 1813, pp. 49-50.

[39]Lucas, op. cit., p. 14; William F. Coffin, 1812: The War, and
Its Moral, (Montreal, 1864), p. 92.

distracted situation which the war had created. He hoped to found a

seminary in Glengarry for the education and training of a local clergy.

Such a project would, of course, aid substantially the growth of the

Catholic Church in Upper Canada, and at the same time keep its develop-

ment firmly under Macdonell's control. But he could hardly appeal to

British officials for the necessary financial support on these grounds.

The services of himself and the Catholics of Glengarry during the war

would be offered in evidence. To ensure the reconstruction of the

province within the Empire this loyal foundation should be expanded

and strengthened. Thus, he appealed to Prevost for help in raising

the Seminary on the ground that

> Such an institution would be of all other means the best
> calculated to instill on the susceptible minds of youth
> the genuine principles of the British constitution, and
> guard them against the contagion of democracy and
> irreligion so rapidly diffusing through every part of the
> Province by the necessary intercourse of the lower order
> of our people with the emigrants and adventurers from
> the United States.[40]

Precisely because of this "necessary intercourse of the lower

order of our people", it was equally important to have the clergy on

the government payroll, as Macdonell indicated to Lord Sidmouth:

> Allowing that the Catholics of this Province were
> sufficiently able both to educate and maintain their
> clergy, as few men can properly support their authority
> over those on whom they depend for their livelihood,
> and still fewer however pure their principles, and
> disinterested their views will feel so cordially
> attached to a Government from which they derive no
> immediate benefit.[41]

---

[40] P A C., Upper Canada Sundries, Macdonell to Prevost, December 1814.

[41] Ibid., Macdonell to Sidmouth, 20 December 1814.

Loyalty, to Macdonell, was no abstract virtue in this case, but rather a function of the necessary interdependence of church and state. In his opinion, the warmth of response of the Upper Canadian population to the demands of the war--which had varied widely across the province-- only gave point to his contentions. The more independent and authoritative the position of the clergy, the better able they were to elicit a favourable reaction from their congregations in aid of the government.

Sir Gordon Drummond, the Administrator of the Canadas, saw considerable merit in the priest's arguments. He cordially supported Macdonell's solicitations of the Colonial Office, and in his lengthy supporting letter he remarked that:

> The character of this gentleman is too well known and too long established as appear by the documents [sic] which accompany his memorial to require much eulogium from me. Suffice it to say I consider him worthy of Your Lordship's notice, and his proposals for establishing the means of educating the Scotch Catholic Population in Upper Canada by the assistance of a few native Clergymen and Schoolmasters of that persuasion merit, I conceive, Your Lordship's attention.
>
> . . . it is but bare justice to say that the statement made in his memorial of Mr. McDonell's exertions and services during the late war with America is strictly correct, and that I am persuaded the most beneficial effects were, on may occations [sic] experienced from them.[42]

Drummond also recommended that Macdonell's personal salary be increased; which it was, to £100, "as a testimony of the sense entertained by His

---

[42]P.A.C., CO42, vol. 374, Drummond to Lord Bathurst (Colonial Secretary), 10 July 1815; copy also in A.A.K., Macdonell Papers.

Royal Highness of the services which he has rendered to the Province".[43]

If Macdonell was gratified by this indication of royal favour, his pleasure would be modified by the knowledge that the fortunes of that other churchman, with whose career his own would so often come in contact, were advancing even more rapidly. In a tone that was somewhat patronizing, John Strachan wrote from the provincial capital informing Macdonell that he had "just seen the Governor who delivered the Prince Regent's mandamus appointing me an honorary Member of the Executive Council so that if you remain as good a Catholic as you have done for so many years I may be able to be of use to you . . . ."[44] There is no reason, however, to doubt Strachan's sincerity at that time. He had just concluded the preparation of a report on the state of religion in Upper Canada for the Chief Justice. It was presented then to the Administrator, Sir Gordon Drummond, and included the observation that:

> In that Scotch settlement in the Eastern District there is
> a Clergyman of the Church of Scotland [John Bethune] and
> a Catholic Priest [Macdonell] both of whom are men of
> great merit. They receive each ₤50 from Govt.--an
> allowance which ought to be increased.[45]

Yet, they were both ambitious men. While they treated each other with

---

[43] P.A.C., C042, vol. 157, Yorke to Macdonell, 10 January 1815. Macdonell, as a chaplain. was not eligible for half pay, but he was granted special consideration by the government.

[44] G.W. Spragge (ed.), The John Strachan Letter Book: 1812-34, (Toronto, 1946), Strachan to Macdonell, 25 September 1815, pp. 91-92. The occasion of the letter, apparently, was a rumour that the capital might be removed to Kingston; and Strachan was inquiring about the purchase of some land which Macdonell had there.

[45] P.A.C., John Strachan Papers, Letter Book 1, microfilm reel 10; see also Spragge, op. cit., pp. 74-75. The report is dated 1 March 1815.

great cordiality, and there was a real affection between them, their relationship was marked by a constant wariness. Macdonell, especially, felt that Strachan would and did use his position on occasion to thwart his plans. But if his satisfaction was thus tempered, he had little time to dwell upon it. The aftermath of the war would also bring a substantial change in his career: a change that would enlarge his opportunity to play a leading role on the Upper Canadian scene, and at the same time increase his usefulness to the government of the province.

IV

On June 1, 1816, the small Catholic community of Kingston was able to witness a quite unusual scene. Bishop J.O. Plessis had arrived to consecrate the first Catholic Church in the town.[46] For Macdonell, it marked the beginning of his long association with the city which would become his episcopal see. It would be some time yet before he left Glengarry to take up his residence in Kingston, but the historical memory of the city has adopted him thoroughly.[47] Indeed, there was little need for a church in Kingston until the end of the war. There were few Catholics, and Macdonell had regarded it as a mission station.

---

[46]"Report of the Visitation of Bishop Plessis, June 3, 1816", cited in R. Preston, (ed.), Kingston Before the War of 1812, (Toronto, 1959), p.c., n. 144.

[47]"At Chateauguay, de Salaberry with his Voltigeurs, supported by a company of Glengarry Light Infantry, defeated an American force five times their number. It was gratifying to Kingstonians to know that Father Macdonell and his Fencibles had distinguished themselves in the fighting." James A. Roy, Kingston: The King's Town, (Toronto, 1952), p. 95.

When Catholic services were held, it was in the Anglican St. George's Church.[48]

But Plessis had other than routine ecclesiastical interests in visiting Macdonell. He now thought the time propitious to make a determined attempt to secure British agreement to the division of the Diocese of Quebec. The Bishop had been apprised that Macdonell was planning a trip to England to solicit support for his seminary, and to persuade the British authorities to provide financial aid to Catholic clergymen and school masters. Macdonell was charged by Plessis to act as his agent, and use his influence with the Colonial Office to secure official sanction for the division.[49] Thus, twelve years after he had departed, Macdonell set out for Britain on his two-fold mission.

On his way, Macdonell visited the Maritime colonies, and at Antigonish he met with Fathers MacEachern, Gaulin and Burke, who, like himself were all future bishops in British North America. Together, they probably discussed the best manner in which Plessis' instructions could be carried out.[50] In the fall, he sailed for England, and took up residence in London where he began his protracted negotiations with Lord Bathurst, the Colonial Secretary. It would be necessary to convince Bathurst that a division of the diocese would be in the interest of the

---

[48]See E.E. Horsey, Kingston, unpublished manuscript, Queen's University Archives, Kingston; (Kingston, 1932), p. 139.

[49]Documents cited in Lucien Lemieux, L'Etablissement de la Premiére Province Ecclésiastique au Canada 1783-1844; (Montreal, 1968), p. 93.

[50]A.A. Johnston, A History of the Catholic Church in Eastern Nova Scotia, (Antigonish, 1960), pp. 333-34.

government, and not just a convenient solution to the physical problems involved in the administration of so immense a territory.

Macdonell's major argument was that such a decentralization would bind the new Vicars-Apostolic (the creation of which the proposed division would entail) to the British Government. As he put it; "It is self evident that appointments of this nature ought to proceed from Great Britain in order to have every possible tie upon the Colonies that could bind them to the Parent Country".[51] Bathurst was prepared to concede the necessity of creating new bishoprics, but he was more reluctant to accord official recognition to Plessis as Bishop of Quebec--which presumably would place him on the same footing as the Anglican Bishop-- and recommend him for a seat in the Legislative Council. To Macdonell, however, this was simply the logical result of British policy toward Catholics in British North America which began with the Quebec Act of 1774. In the end, Macdonell prevailed.[52] Assured by him that Plessis was eagerly in favor, Bathurst explained to Sir John Sherbrooke, the new Governor-in-Chief in Canada, that:

> . . . having understood distinctly from [Macdonell] in
> reply to the enquiries which I thought it necessary to
> make on that subject that the proposed measure had
> received the entire concurrence and approbation of the
> Roman Catholic Bishop himself I thought it my duty to
> recommend to Lord Castlereagh such a communication with
> the Secretary of State for the Pope.[53]

---

[51] P.A.C., CO42, Vol. 360, Macdonell to Bathurst, 16 January 1817.

[52] Lemieux, op. cit., p. 94. Lemieux argues that Macdonell's presence in London, and his influence at the Colonial Office were crucial to the success of Plessis' initiative.

[53] P.A.C., G1, Despatches from the Colonial Office, 1791-1841, vol. 9, Bathurst to Sherbrooke, 4 June 1817.

The Colonial Secretary also decided to recommend Macdonell as Vicar-Apostolic for Upper Canada should his advice be followed.[54]

On Bathurst's recommendation, Lord Castlereagh opened communication with the Papacy which was awaiting British approval.

> Understanding that a Proposition has been submitted to the Pope by the Roman Catholic Bishop of Canada recommending the separation of the Provinces of Upper Canada, Nova Scotia and Prince Edward's Island from the Diocese of Quebec, and the appointment of a Vicar-Apostolic in each of those Provinces, I have availed myself of this circumstance to acquaint Your Eminence that His Majesty's Government will view such an arrangement with satisfaction, and at the same time I beg to submit to Your Eminence that H.R.H. the Prince Regent would feel gratified that the choice of His Holiness of Persons to fill those high situations should fall upon the Revd A. Macdonell as Vicar-Apostolic of Upper Canada, upon the Revd [blank] Burke as Vicar-Apostolic of Nova Scotia, and upon the Revd Aneas MacEchran [sic] as Vicar Apostolic of Prince Edward's Island.[55]

In due time, the Vatican replied to Castlereagh's overture and announced that:

> . . . His Holiness, who, having already resolved upon the erection of an Apostolic Vicariate in Nova Scotia, has charged the Congregation of the Propaganda to carry into effect immediately the above scheme in all its bearings.
>
> I now have the pleasure to acquaint Y.E. that H. Holiness has already gratified the desires of H.R.H. by the choice of Apostolic Vicars for Nova Scotia and Upper Canada, which has fallen on Messrs. Edmund Burke and Macdonell, who were already abundantly known to him.[56]

---

[54] A.A.K., Macdonell Papers, Goulburn to Macdonell, 24 January 1817. Henry Goulburn was, at the time, Under-Secretary for War and the Colonies.

[55] P.A.C., MG12, C8, Supplementary II, 95, Vol. 423, Castlereagh to Cardinal Consalvi, private, 30 April 1817.

[56] Ibid., F.O. 43, Vol. 10, Consalvi to Castlereagh, 6 October 1817.

The niceties of the diplomatic correspondence do not disguise what, in fact, was a very delicate problem. Despite the religious situation in England, the British Government was according official recognition to Catholicism in British North America. Macdonell, by urging the British officials to initiate discussion with the Vatican, created the illusion that it was a British decision. The Vatican, realizing that any overt act on its part would be unwelcome, could thus respond to the British proposal along lines which it had already approved. Altogether, it was a rather neat solution to a somewhat thorny problem.

Concurrently, Macdonell was apparently meeting some success in the other object of his journey to England--financial support for the church in Upper Canada. He based his request, as usual, on the past and potential utility to the government of such a scheme. Pointing to the established loyalty of the Gaelic-speaking, Catholic Highlanders, the priest argued that it was a product of their cultural cohesiveness which ought to be encouraged. "Thus secured by the double barrier of their language and religion they might for a long time stand proof against the contagious politics of their democratical neighbours."[57] His proposed seminary would also be responsible for developing an elite group within the Catholic community:

> It is my intention to establish the principal school at my place of Residence in the County of Glengarry, in order to be under my own Superintendence and direction, and for this school I wish to procure a few masters in

---

[57]P.A.C., CO42, Vol. 360, Macdonell to Bathurst, 16 January 1817.

> this country of Superior talents and learning capable
> of educating gentlemen's sons upon a more liberal and
> extensive plan than what would be necessary for the
> lower classes of settlers.[58]

Such an advanced education would, of course, prepare Catholics to take

leading positions in the political life of Upper Canada. The fact was

not lost upon Macdonell that the former pupils of John Strachan--such

as John Beverley Robinson--were now assuming senior positions in the

provincial government. When entrenched with Strachan himself, the

opportunities for mischief would be manifold, should they determine

to thwart Macdonell's pretensions for the Roman Catholic Church.

Macdonell could not, however, confide in Bathurst in this matter.

Rather, he felt it necessary to take the highest ground in justifying

his application to the Colonial Secretary. It was on the level of imperial

policy that Britain would reap the benefit if the Colonial Office accepted

his arguments and granted his request. Loyal Catholics would people

and strengthen the Empire. Even with only meagre assistance, he wrote,

> I have been enabled so effecutally to direct to our own
> colonies the destination of Scotch Catholics, who have
> been under the necessity of quitting their own Country,
> that since that period not one of them has emigrated to
> the United States, altho during the same space of time
> thousands of Scotch Presbyterians, and innumerable
> Irish Catholics have found their way to that country,
> who would have proved excellent subjects in the British
> Colonies, and that those were not only lost forever to
> their native Country, but became its most formidable,
> and inveterate enemies, and swelled the ranks of American
> armies in their late attempts to conquer the Canadas, as
> will be certified by every British officer employed
> during that time in those Provinces.[59]

---

[58] Ibid.

[59] Ibid.

The obvious conclusion that the Colonial Secretary was expected to draw was, of course, that given adequate means, Macdonell would ensure, at least for Catholics, the creation in Upper Canada of a politically and socially stable community upon whose loyalty the British government could depend.

The effective accomplishment of this objective presumed that Bathurst would authorize the funds requested. There was now a need for haste as well, since the pace of immigration quickened after the war. Disturbed by Bathurst's apparent hesitation, Macdonell became more importunate as the months passed.

> . . . as the danger of infection from the Democratical Principles of their neighbours would necessarily increase in proportion to their growing numbers, and the range of country over which they spread themselves, I consider it my duty to impress on my Lord Bathurst and you, Sir, the necessity of furnishing the means to secure them from that danger. I have already stated . . . that in employing teachers who should be connected with Government by their interest as well as by their principles, appeared to me as the means best calculated for that important end.[60]

With this, Macdonell made his point, at least partially. Bathurst minuted the letter, indicating that he was in agreement with the proposal for teachers' salaries and that he would give the necessary authorization for their payment from Upper Canadian revenues.[61] Macdonell had to content himself with this incomplete achievement. He would have much preferred to have the salaries paid by the home government, and not

---

[60]A.A.K., Macdonell Papers, Macdonell to Goulburn, 12 May 1817.

[61]P.A.C., CO42, Macdonell to Goulburn, 12 May 1817; Minute by Bathurst.

be obliged to rely on the officials at York with whome he was as yet
unsure of his influence. He covered his disappointment in an extravagant
letter of thanks in the name of the Catholics of Upper Canada, promising
that he would "not fail to impress deeply on their minds the value of
this important concession to them, at a moment when so many other demands
are made upon the public purse".[62] Just prior to his return to Upper
Canada, Macdonell forwarded Bathurst's orders for payment of the
salaries to Samuel Smith, the Administrator of the Province.[63]

V

On balance the journey could be reckoned a success. He had the
promise of the Colonial Secretary that his plans for Catholic education
would receive the financial backing of the provincial government. The
question of salaries for Catholic clergymen was, at least, still open.
His petition for an increase in his own salary was now before Lord
Bathurst who would, Macdonell hoped, take a sympathetic view.[64]

His mission for Bishop Plessis had succeeded in every detail.
The Diocese of Quebec had been divided with the sanction of the British
Government; and Vicars Apostolic designated by Britain of whom Plessis
and the Vatican had approved beforehand. He, himself, could shortly
expect to receive official confirmation of his elevation to the episcopal

---

[62] Ibid., Macdonell to Goulburn, 9 June 1817.

[63] P.A.C., Upper Canada Sundries, Macdonell to Smith, 27 September 1817.

[64] A.A.K., Macdonell Papers, Petition to Colonial Secretary, June 1817.

dignity. It would not, perhaps, be untoward to regard it as a mark

of approbation for his exertions in Upper Canada in peace and war

over thirteen years. Yet, would it be so regarded in Upper Canada?

Would his position and influence be consequently enhanced? Or rather,

would it excite a feeling of resentment in Archdeacon Strachan, the

new Executive Councillor, and those members of the government who shared

his views on the proper role of religion in Upper Canada? Macdonell

would have to await the event to gauge how his mission would be inter-

preted by the local authorities.

The situation at York would be confused, as well, by that re-

curring disturbance of colonial political life, the appointment of a new

Lieutenant Governor. So much would depend on his favour. Macdonell's

relations with Francis Gore, and the various military leaders during

the war, had been quite cordial, and in many ways rewarding. But he

had been inclined to rely more upon officials in England in matters of

importance; and put his faith in their capacity to control affairs in

the colony. Yet as Upper Canada grew in population and wealth, so the

scope and power of the government at York increased. Macdonell would

be obliged to turn more and more to the officials there. Sir Peregrine

Maitland, the incoming Lieutenant Governor, would have to be cultivated.

If he were uneasy about the future, Macdonell could be assured

that his success in dealing with the Colonial Office would be noted in

Upper Canada. In the immediate post-war period he was emerging as a

prominent figure in the province. His staunch conservatism, and his

well-publicized services during the war, should make him an obvious but-

tress of the government. And Macdonell had the skill and determination to operate effectively within the social and political parameters of Upper Canada. The government would find him as willing an ally in peace as in war; but one who would expect to be compensated in the political coin of the period.

CHAPTER III

THE MAITLAND YEARS

I

When Macdonell returned to Upper Canada in the late autumn of
1817, he became absorbed for several months in resuming the administrative direction of the church in Upper Canada. His correspondence
of the time reveals an optimism for the future, now buttressed by
Bathurst's assurance of financial aid. Yet, there was disquiet too,
as the months passed and nothing was heard from York as to the manner
in which the promised salaries would be disbursed. The anxiety would
soon turn to suspicion that efforts were being made at the capital to
undo the success he had achieved on his recent journey to England.
Macdonell was well aware of the extent to which events turned on
personal influence in a colonial society such as Upper Canada.

The advent of a new Lieutenant Governor always upset the matrix
of power relationships in the province. In the system of patronage
politics which prevailed, his influence was decisive. It would be
necessary for Macdonell to establish a connection with the new incumbent, Sir Peregrine Maitland, as quickly as possible. The Bishop
could hope to benefit from the conservative reaction in Upper Canada
which followed the Treaty of Ghent. His credentials were impeccable.

But would this be enough, removed as he was from the seat of government and unable to participate in the round of activity at the capital?

The war had, as well, marked a violent intrusion of the outside world into the life of the province. Henceforth, Upper Canada's affairs would be considered in the Imperial context, in London as well as in North America. A proposed union of Upper and Lower Canada, heavy immigration and an apprehensive awareness of the province's 'peculiar position' beside its bustling southern neighbour bedeviled the developing society. In attempting to cope with this rapidly changing situation, the more influential advisors of the new Lieutenant Governor at York felt compelled to exercise a close control over the political, economic and social maturation of the province. If, as Professor Gerald Craig has argued, the design of this tightly-knit group led by John Strachan and John Beverley Robinson was not ignoble, it demanded a persistent vigilance over the increasingly complex life of Upper Canada.[1] To be given effect it also required a Lieutenant Governor sympathetic to their objectives, and loci of support throughout the province. It was during the Maitland years that this 'Family Compact' made its most substantial impact on the life of Upper Canada. They were never able to exercise the same commanding influence over his successor, Sir John Colborne.

Alexander Macdonell was not a member of this Family Compact in the strict sense. While he shared their determination to maintain the

---

[1] Gerald Craig, op. cit., pp. 107-110.

connection with the mother country, and its obverse, their fear of
republicanism; he could not accept the full range of ideological and
institutional bulwarks they sought to erect. Thus he was with them
but not of them. To the extent that Macdonell could be useful to the
ruling group politically, they were prepared to accord him a limited
advantage in the patronage system. Yet as leader of the Roman Catholic
community, he was a threat to their attempt to have the Church of
England accepted as the established church of Upper Canada; a necessary
step, in their view, in ensuring the integrity and security of the
province.

The Maitland years were thus crucial for Macdonell. He could
hope, in his turn, to use the influence of the Compact group to the
advantage of his church. But conscious of the fundamental disagreement
on the question of establishment, he knew there were clear limits to
the gains he could expect. These limits would depend, to a great
extent, on his capacity to create in the minds of that influential
group an image of himself as a reliable and valuable supporter of conservative rule. Their mutual dependence would allow Macdonell considerable scope in the pursuit of his own objectives. He hoped, also,
that he could rely on his growing credit with the Colonial Office to
offset any disadvantage he might encounter in his dealings with the
provincial government. He would not consciously play one off against
the other, but his abiding faith in the Crown would prompt him to
appeal directly to London when he felt it necessary.

II

John Strachan, soon to be Archdeacon, had heard the reports of
Macdonell's apparently fruitful visit to England with considerable mis-
giving. He was quite incensed that such encouragement should be extended by the British Government to any denomination but the Church
of England; not only in principle but because, as he argued, the number
of Catholics in Upper Canada scarcely justified such an increase in
the number of priests and schoolmasters. He complained to the Anglican
Bishop of Quebec that Macdonell "intends to establish a College for
the education of Catholic Priests and the dissemination of Popery.
The object is evidently proselytism and unhappily they have become
rather successful. Add to this My Lord that it is whispered about
that Mr. McDonell is to be created Catholic Bishop of Upper Canada".[2]
It is not unlikely that Strachan's discomfiture was tinged with
jealousy, since he himself was hoping for a mitre if the Anglican
Diocese of Quebec should be divided. His strategic position as a
member of the Executive Council, however, afforded him the opportunity
of delaying the appropriation of funds upon which Macdonell was
relying. Indeed, it would be seven years before Bathurst's promise of
salaries for Catholic teachers and schoolmasters would be fully redeemed.
At bottom, the explanation for this long delay reveals both the manner
in which the Compact exercised control over the Province, and the
degree to which it was necessary for the conservative elements in the
society to sustain each other. It illustrates, as well, the nature of

---

[2]P.A.C., Strachan Papers, Strachan to Bishop of Quebec, 10 November
1817, microfilm, reel 10, p. 175.

the relationship of these two ambitious and talented churchmen.

It is true that Macdonell and Strachan respected each other; indeed, that there was a substantial degree of affection between them. But it was a respect that might exist between two skilled gladiators; and an affection that was bred by the knowledge that they had mutual enemies and might be of service to one another. There was never a genuine openness and frankness between them; nor was their friendship based on the bed-rock of absolute convictions, completely shared. As much as they held similar views of the ideal Upper Canadian society and polity, there was a fundamental distinction between John Strachan and Alexander Macdonell. Each of them believed that he was the leader of the legally established church of the Province. Strachan took his stand on the Constitutional Act of 1791; Macdonell took his on the Quebec Act. And like Martin Luther, they were both aware that true belief was a burden that could neither be shared nor compromised.

This wariness which existed between them led Macdonell to suspect that it was probably Strachan who was obstructing the payment of the salaries. The former would have much preferred to receive the funds from the home government and thus be independent of the provincial authorities. It would be difficult for him to put it quite so boldly; so when he complained to Lord Bathurst that the promised salaries had not been paid, he argued that "it would be very desirable, that the public functionaries of Religion in this Province should depend rather on His Majesty's Government than upon their hearers for their subsistence, and I now beg leave to press that idea on your Lordship's

attention more earnestly than ever".[3] In his minute on the letter,
the Colonial Secretary regretted the delay, and indicated that should
the Provincial Government fail to pay the salaries, the British Government would fulfil the pledge. Macdonell was so informed by Henry
Goulburn, the Under-Secretary.[4]

Despite this reassurance, Macdonell heard nothing further on
the matter for two years. He sought the intervention of Bishop Plessis,
the Duke of Richmond, who was then Governor-in-Chief, and of Lieutenant
Governor Maitland, all with little effect. Maitland, in fact, had
informed Bathurst that the whole unfortunate business was the fault of
a balky Assembly which refused to authorize the funds.[5] The division
of the Catholic diocese of Quebec, meanwhile, had taken place, and the
Pope's Bull arrived creating Macdonell Bishop of Upper Canada,
suffragan to Bishop Plessis of Quebec.[6] He was, he wrote to Plessis,
in no position to be consecrated.

> Without the command of as much money as would defray the
> expenses of my journey to Quebec, where am I to look for
> the necessary supplies to support myself in a new and
> necessarily more expensive situation, since the Government
> at home have come to a determination not to fulfil their
> engagements to me and the Government of this Province
> through the jealousy and prejudices of certain members of
> the Council continue to use all the means in their power
> to disappoint me.[7]

-----

[3]P.A.C., CO42, Vol. 361, Macdonell to Bathurst, 26 May 1818.

[4]A.A.K., Macdonell Papers, Goulburn to Macdonell, 6 August 1818.

[5]P.A.C., CO42, Vol. 362, Maitland to Bathurst, 6 December 1819.
See also, R.A.Q., 1928-29, Correspondence of Bishop Plessis, Plessis to
Macdonell, 19 December 1818.

[6]His ecclesiastical title was Bishop of Rhesina, in partibus infidelium

[7]A.A.K., Macdonell Papers, Macdonell to Plessis, 3 October 1820.

Macdonell now seemed convinced that it was Strachan and his friends who were frustrating the disbursement of funds authorized by Bathurst. Learning of his suspicions, Strachan wrote to the new Bishop to indicate how hurt he was that Macdonell should suspect him. "I must begin by remarking that I am getting too old to lose friends by any faults of my own, and would therefore go out of my way to clear up and correct rumours than hasard such a result."[8] Strachan went on to complain that he was having difficulty securing salaries for his own clergymen. Quite unpersuaded, Macdonell replied rather tartly,

> That there is a fault somewhere cannot be denied; that I am perhaps the most improper person in the world to find out where the fault lies may be allowed, and in my state of perplexity, and distraction of mind it would hardly be wondered that I should reflect on my friends who had every-thing to say in the Government of the Province since my views began to be thwarted.
>
> I am glad however to find that I was mistaken, and I hope to have soon still more convincing proofs of my error when I shall have the pleasure of visiting York, and meeting my friends, by the facility that will be afforded me of obtaining my just and reasonable demands.[9]

Though he closed the letter with "warm regards to Mrs. Strachan and the children", Macdonell knew his man. Two weeks later, the Archdeacon wrote the Lord Bishop of Quebec.

> When the Ministry were so favourable to the Catholics especially to the Rev. Mc. McDonell of Glengarry in making him a titular bishop and ordering salaries for three clergymen and three or four Catholic teachers the despatch to this Government did not specify the mode of payment. Luckily there was no fund from which it could be taken and when the matter was mentioned I considered it my duty to insist upon the payment of four Established

---

[8] P.A.C., _Strachan Papers_, Strachan to Macdonell, 4 September 1820.

[9] A.A.K., _Macdonell Papers_, Macdonell to Strachan, 1 November 1820.

clergymen who had always been paid out of the revenue of
this Province. Mr. McDonell had been indefatigable in the
business but has hitherto failed and now it is reported
that he means to bring the matter before the Legislature.[10]

In fact, Macdonell would have to make another journey to England
in 1824 before the matter was settled satisfactorily. The drawn-out
affair indicates that when the vital interests of religion were involved,
they treated each other extremely gingerly to say the least. The issue,
in the Upper Canadian context, was simply too important for either of
them to be caught off guard. They might act in unison to denounce the
pretensions and aspirations of the evangelical denominations--after all,
they were mostly American Methodists. Yet they could never relax in
their attitudes toward each other. Strachan saw Macdonell and Upper
Canadian Catholics as a potential challenge to the position of the Church
of England which he was so anxious to secure. Macdonell, for his part,
viewed Strachan's machinations as a wicked attempt to deny to the Catholics
their just rights. Yet, important as this disagreement was, it did not
prevent Macdonell seeking, and the Government conceding to him, a place
in the web of influence and favours which bound together the conservative
forces of the province.

Lieutenant Governor Sir Peregrine Maitland had barely time to
become settled in his new position when Macdonell made contact with him.
The occasion was the formation of the Highland Society of Canada, and
many of the original members were partners and senior officials of the
North West Company. The Bishop had been instrumental in securing a

---

[10]P.A.C., Strachan Papers, Strachan to Bishop of Quebec, 13
November 1820. Spragge's edition of Strachan's correspondence dates
this letter 19 February 1821, for some unexplained reason.

charter from the Royal Highland Society of London.[11] He informed the
inaugural meeting that he "had obtained the consent of His Excellency
Sir Peregrine Maitland, to be elected the First President".[12] Macdonell
was not above trading on the sentimental attachment of most Scots for
their homeland. He himself became the first vice-president of the
Society. The strong personal ties that he had cultivated with the
partners of the North West Company served him in a variety of ways.
Indeed, Thomas Thain, one of the partners in the company, was at that
time covering his loans from the Montreal Bank.[13]

The connection, as well, made him the link between the Quebec
hierarchy and the Company. Plessis was hoping to introduce missionaries
into Red River and the Athabaska country, but Macdonell was not at all
encouraging. The relationship between the Nor'westers and the Hudson's
Bay Company was extremely tense just prior to the merger of 1821.
Macdonell's partiality was clear as he informed Plessis that McGillivray

> would not afford either aid or support to the Clergymen
> connected with the Settlement of the Red River except
> what common civilities would demand, and I have every
> reason to suppose he has not altered his opinion, because
> he considers that settlement formed not only in opposi-
> tion, but with the avowed intention of undermining and
> upsetting the North West Company, consequently of ruining
> forever him and his friends.[14]

He advised his superior to defer any further initiatives in the west

---

[11]P.A.C., Simon McGillivray Papers, Vol. 6, p. 10

[12]Ibid., p. 29. P.A.C., Upper Canada Sundries, Macdonell to Major Hillier (Secretary to Maitland), 17 November 1818.

[13]A.A.K., Macdonell Papers, Macdonell to Thain, 25 June 1820.

[14]Ibid., Macdonell to Plessis, 25 March 1821.

until the anticipated union of the two companies should take place. After that, he suggested, conditions might be more favourable.[15] Both Macdonell and Strachan were involved to some extent in the tangled affair of the great fur-trading rivalry; indeed, the latter had quarrelled seriously with Lord Selkirk.[16] Both, however, supported the merger as the only solution to what they considered an intractable problem.[17]

The Scottish connection had provided Macdonell with a means of establishing himself with Maitland; and his influence in the Eastern District had become such that the Lieutenant Governor looked upon him as an effective agent of local control. As he put it to the Colonial Secretary, in his laconic manner, ". . . with respect to Mr. Macdonell himself, I have every reason to regard him as a good subject of His Majesty, and usefully active in promoting the views of Government".[18] The utility, of course, demanded a quid pro quo. In June 1819, Maitland appointed Macdonell to the Land Board of the Eastern District.[19] Since land was the greatest single asset of the young province, it was a

[15] Ibid., Macdonell to Plessis, 6 May 1821. R.A.Q., 1828-29, Plessis Correspondence, Plessis to Macdonell, 13 August 1821.

[16] P.A.C., Strachan Papers, Strachan to Dr. Brown, 1 December 1818.

[17] Ibid., Strachan to [?]   , 27 July 1818. A.A.K., Macdonell Papers, Macdonell to Plessis, 6 May 1821.

[18] P.A.C., CO42, Vol. 362, Maitland to Bathurst, 6 December 1819.

[19] P.A.C., Upper Canada Sundries, Macdonell to Hillier, 16 June 1819: See also ibid., Alexander Macdonell (location agent in the Eastern District) to Hillier, 7 June 1819, in which he indicates that the Bishop has control of the appropriation of land in the township of Caledonia; and also Kingston Chronicle, 9 July 1819.

matter of considerable importance to have a voice in its allocation.
Not only would it enable him to forward the interests of his people in
the District, but this public recognition by the government would
enhance his authority and influence.

Maitland had also asked Macdonell to serve on a committee inves-
tigating the purchase of Indian lands from the time of the conquest.[20]
In 1821, the Bishop was appointed to a special commission which directly
concerned the interests of the people of Glengarry. For some years the
boundary between Upper and Lower Canada had been subject to some dispute
between settlers in the Eastern District and the westernmost seigniory
of Lower Canada. Macdonell had, in the past, complained of alleged
encroachments upon the lands of his flock. The authorities of Lower
Canada suggested a joint commission to resolve the difficulty. Major
Hillier wrote to Macdonell that

> it has occurred to the Lieut. Governor that he could not
> appoint to this commission any person better qualified
> for its due execution in all respects, than yourself,
> provided it be agreeable to you to undertake it. In
> this case, as there are in your part of the country
> several well qualified Surveyors of whose relative
> merit you perhaps can best judge, His Excellency would
> be happy that you recommended one for the service. I
> shall be happy to hear from you at your earliest
> leasure [sic] and to know when you could conveniently
> attend to the objict [sic] in question.[21]

Macdonell responded to this overture with alacrity, for not only
did it manifest his growing connection with the provincial government,
but allowed him direct patronage and would help to consolidate his

---

[20] P.A.C., Upper Canada Sundries, Macdonell to Hillier, 21 May 1821.

[21] A.A.K., Macdonell Papers, Hillier to Macdonell, 10 October 1821.

position in his District. In his rather effusive acknowledgement, he

told Hillier that

> I am fully sensible of the honor His Excellency does me
> in inviting me to act as a Commissioner in establishing
> the boundary line between the two provinces, as I con-
> sider such an appointment a mark of confidence His
> Excellency is pleased to place in me. I feel most
> grateful to Sir Peregrine for his kind condescension
> in interesting himself in this business which I took
> the liberty of mentioning to His Excellency on more
> occasions than one.[22]

Included in the reply was his recommendation of David Thompson, the

explorer of the Pacific Coast ten years earlier, for the position of

Surveyor of the boundary. This was only one of many suggestions he

made for appointments to positions in the administration and militia,

hoping to capitalize on what he felt was his now established link with

the Lieutenant Governor.[23] It was not surprising that he should assume

his recommendations would carry weight with Maitland, for even the

vexing problem of the salaries for the schoolmasters was partially

solved by Maitland's intervention. The provincial appropriations for

1822 included provision for their payment, although there was no mention

of the arrears which Macdonell was still determined to collect if at all

possible.[24] This is not to say that he was becoming more dependent on

---

[22] P.A.C., Upper Canada Sundries, Macdonell to Hillier, 26 October 1821.

[23] P.A.C., ibid., Macdonell to Hillier, 28 April 1820, 12 September 1820, 30 October 1820, 8 March 1821. One of his more interesting proposals concerned his cousin Miles Macdonell, the former governor of Assiniboia, for sheriff of the Ottawa District on 26 November 1821. Three months later he withdrew it on the grounds that he suspected Miles' mental stability.

[24] Ibid., Macdonell to Maitland, 25 June 1822. A.A.K., Macdonell Papers, Macdonell to Hillier, 23 March 1823 in which the Bishop sends his thanks to Maitland for the salaries, ". . . to be distributed at my discretion".

the Upper Canadian Government in his attitude. While he was prepared to accept assistance from that source, he would have preferred the aid to come from England. As he had put it to Hillier, "I would much rather have those under my charge consider themselves indebted for any favor their good conduct deserve, to the gracious bounty of their Sovereign than to the liberality of the Provincial Assembly".[25] Macdonell believed that the Colonial Office was the more important and more secure source of power and influence. This was partly borne out in 1822 when he applied to Maitland for a land grant to which he claimed entitlement for militia service during the war. Maitland was concerned that it would set an awkward precedent since he did not regard chaplains eligible for militia grants. Bathurst granted the request anyway, ". . . to be complied with an account of the special services of Dr. M. and not on account of his situation as Chaplain".[26] Yet, Macdonell could not be unaware that as Upper Canada grew in population and in the complexity of its affairs more and more of the vital decisions would be made in the provincial capital. Maitland, for his part, remained concerned with protecting the position of the Church of England and its advantages, but recognized as well the need to maintain agencies of political and social control over a Province growing ever more heterogeneous.[27]

---

[25] Ibid., Macdonell to Hillier, 16 May 1819.

[26] P.A.C., CO42, Vol. 368, Maitland to Bathurst, 18 March 1822; minute by Bathurst.

[27] See F.M. Quealey, "The Administration of Sir Peregrine Maitland in Upper Canada, 1818-1828", unpublished Ph.D. thesis, University of Toronto, 1968; passim.

Lieutenant Governor Maitland's increasing willingness to accommodate Macdonell seems to have been influenced by two interrelated
factors; the latter's elevation to the rank of Vicar-Apostolic, and the
heavy immigration into the Province of Irish Catholics in the early
1820's. There was some concern that they would be difficult to incorporate into Upper Canadian life. Their arrival, in fact, provided
the occasion for Macdonell to petition for an increase in his salary
on the ground

> That the turbulent disposition and want of subordination
> among the Irish Emigrants have already been attended with
> great difficulties and trouble to your memorialist in
> tranquilizing and reducing them to order and regularity,
> having been under the painful necessity of dismissing
> already no less than four of the Priests who followed
> them to this Province whose principles and moral conduct
> was [sic] such as not to be tolerated.[28]

The Lieutenant Governor forwarded the application with his approval; and
in addition, because he felt such an increase would be justified to
enable Macdonell to support the new dignity of Bishop of Upper Canada.[29]

His new ecclesiastical position, however, was becoming as much
a source of worry as gratification. Macdonell had originally hoped,
as had Bishop Plessis, that the division of the Diocese of Quebec would
be complete; that he would be made Bishop in ordinary, rather than a
Vicar-Apostolic, suffragan to the Bishop of Quebec. From a local
political standpoint, the important question revolved around the right
to appoint and control the priests in the various provinces of British

---

[28] P.A.C., CO42, Vol. 370; enclosure in Maitland to Bathurst,
26 April 1823.

[29] Ibid.

North America. Lord Dalhousie, the Governor of Canada, was especially

conscious of this. He was apprehensive about the quasi-division which

had taken place, and complained to Lord Bathurst that

> It appears that the Catholic Bishop of Quebec has it in
> contemplation at present to gather under his immediate
> control, authority and patronage all those Vicaires
> Apostoliques lately consecrated Bishops by him, and
> thus acquire an influence which till now he had not had.
>
> It was stated to me that much inconvenience and dis-
> satisfaction would arise was the Catholic Bishop of
> Quebec to appoint the inferior clergy in the Provinces
> now committed to the Vicaires Apostoliques in Nova Scotia,
> New Brunswick and Upper Canada. On the other hand,
> that much advantage would be derived by a subdivision
> of them, in committing the superintendance to the
> Vicaire, or Bishop in the Provinces severally.
>
> They would certainly provide proper persons as
> inferior Priests in their Districts.
>
> They would provide them from the British territories.
>
> They would better control the political principles of
> their flock.
>
> Their Priests would be secured against removal at the
> Caprice of the Bishop of Quebec, and what is more important
> than all these considerations it would guard against an
> influence that may soon grow into a form in this country,
> which might not be so easily controlled bye and bye.
>
> I take it for granted that H.M. Government has only to
> express its desire that such subdivisions should be made.[30]

From his vantage point in London, however, the Colonial Secretary

had not agreed. In his reply to Dalhousie, Bathurst indicated that it

was felt that "it could be extremely difficult to establish any control

over four independent bishops". In any case, he continued, he was

satisfied with the conduct of Plessis, even though the latter, and the

---

[30] P.A.C., MG 24, A 12, Dalhousie Papers, Vol. 8, Dalhousie to
Bathurst, 10 July 1821.

Vatican, had urged the division of the See of Quebec. It seemed more important to Bathurst to maintain close control over the hierarchy.

> I need not mention to your Lordship that the Bishop of
> Quebec receives a salary from the Crown; that the
> recognition of his title depends upon his seat in the
> Legislative Council which depends upon the favor of
> the Crown and there are other local arrangements
> conducive to his interest or convenience which cannot
> but make him more or less desirous to be well with
> the government. I might also suggest to your
> Lordship quite confidentially that there are national
> reasons why a bishop of Lower Canada is less likely
> than another to exercise his influence in a manner
> favorable to the United States.

This had been the determining factor in appointing vicars to assist the Bishop of Quebec. His opinion was, however, qualified to the extent that he informed Lord Dalhousie that it would not take long to discover whether this was the better policy. If not, then he would accept Dalhousie's argument and recommend a complete division of the Diocese of Quebec.[31]

There is no direct evidence that Macdonell was advising Dalhousie in this matter. The two were, however, on very good terms. The Governor had, on occasion, gone out of his way to follow Macdonell's wishes especially in regard to land grants.

> The Power to grant in your neighbourhood, being the
> Province of Upper Canada, lies with Sir P. Maitland
> but I have the new Military Settlements in my charge,
> and if the good men of Glengarry choose to go there,
> I will grant them 100 acres in Richmond, Perth, etc.
> under the conditions of immediate settlement. I have
> put this upon paper for your own information that you
> may offer no more than I have in my power to give.[32]

---

[31] P.A.C., Series G. Bathurst to Dalhousie, 10 September 1821; cited in Somers, op. cit., p. 75.

[32] P.A.C., Dalhousie Papers, Dalhousie to Macdonell, 8 January 1821.

Dalhousie had also attempted to help Macdonell in securing the salaries for the priests and teachers, suggesting that they might be paid out of the military chest.[33] The Governor, as well, considered "it a matter of very great importance . . . that the Head of the Catholic Church in each Province should be maintained with respectability and that policy can never be more useful than in the case of Mr. McDonell".[34] Whether the two were working together or not, they would both be pleased if the Diocese should be divided. Dalhousie was most encouraging when Macdonell informed him that he was planning to go to England to try and accomplish in person those objectives which letters and petitions had failed to obtain.

Macdonell had concluded that only a direct personal appeal to Bathurst would resolve the question of arrears of salaries, and relieve him of the burden of debt which had accumulated as a result. The delicate matter of breaking up the See of Quebec could best be handled by quiet negotiation with Bathurst and Rome. In addition, Macdonell was taking a hand in the most burning political question of the day, the proposed union of Upper and Lower Canada. He agreed fully with John Strachan and J.B. Robinson that such a union would not be in the best interests of the upper province. There was however, in his approach, a degree of naivete in dealing with an event of such broad significance despite Macdonell's growing expertise in provincial politics. The

---

[33] Ibid., Dalhousie to Bathurst, 18 January 1821.

[34] Ibid.

government in London had withdrawn the bill at the end of the 1822 session of the British Parliament when it became clear the members wished to have the provinces consulted on so important a matter. John Beverley Robinson, who was in London at the time, had stoutly opposed precipitate action.

Opposition was quickly emerging in both Upper and Lower Canada. Louis-Joseph Papineau, the rising French-Canadian politician, hoped to recruit Macdonell as a delegate to London to urge the government to abandon the proposal. The Bishop declined on the ground of ill health, but indicated that he would be proceeding to London in the spring of 1823 and would lend his support. He was sure he would:

> not be too late for serving the cause in which you are
> embarked, and with so much laudable zeal you seem
> determined to support. Whatever my own opinion may
> be of an Union of the Legislatures of these Provinces
> on a fair and liberal basis I am a determined enemy to
> everything that pervades the liberty of the subject or
> encroaches on the sacred ground of our holy Religion,
> and the very idea of cramming by force a measure down
> the throats of freeborn British subjects is so revolting
> to my own mind, that it gives me a very bad opinion of
> the promoters of the Union to see them proceed with such
> violence. A great proportion of the population of this
> County and of the neighbouring one are adverse to the
> measure, have had meetings and signed petitions to
> oppose it.[35]

Papineau may not have been especially concerned with his position as a "freeborn British subject", but he probably appreciated Macdonell's advice on how to contact influential people in London which the

---

[35]P.A.C., MG 24, B 1, Papineau-Neilson Collection, Vol. 18, Macdonell to Papineau, 6 January 1823. Gerald Craig suggests that commercial interests in the Eastern District supported the union, but Macdonell probably did represent majority opinion accurately. Craig, op. cit., pp. 101-105.

Bishop included.

On the same day he replied to Papineau, he wrote a long letter

of introduction for him to his old friend Lord Sidmouth. In highly

charged terms he described the controversy in Lower Canada, where "both

parties have allowed their passions to hurry them into the opposite

extremes, the [French-Canadians] will not compromise, and the [English

merchants] will not be satisfied with anything less than the degradation

and the political extermination of the Canadians".[36] Despite the

hyperbole, Macdonell was quite concerned with the implications of the

projected union. After a flattering reference to Papineau--an opinion

he would soon change--he went on to sketch the dangers he anticipated

from such a merger.

> I have indeed every reason to apprehend that pressing
> this measure at the present juncture will render [the
> French-Canadians] disaffected to the British Government
> and if their minds be once alienated the consequences
> may be very serious. At present both the Canadas are
> filling fast with Scotch Radicals, Irish rebels and
> American Republicans and it is well known that all
> those are perfectly void of every principle of loyalty
> or attachment to the British Government. Should the
> Canadians get disaffected and join with the others just
> mentioned in attempting to shake off the dependence on
> Great Britain I much fear it would be a difficult matter
> to prevent them.[37]

Macdonell appears to have taken higher ground in opposing the

union than the conservative ruling group in York. They were more con-

cerned with the potential threat it posed to Upper Canada, and to

---

[36]A.A.K., Macdonell Papers, Macdonell to Sidmouth, 6 January
1823. On the same day, he wrote a similar letter of introduction for
Wolfred Neilson to Henry Monteith, M.P. for Glasgow.

[37]Ibid.

their own position. He was, of course, much less intimately involved
in provincial affairs. It may very well have been his fear, however,
that a political union would delay or prevent the separation of Upper
Canada from the See of Quebec; or less disingenuously, his knowledge
of the lower province may have excited a very real apprehension of the
impact of such a union.

In any case, he felt he would soon have an opportunity to bring
his influence to bear. The British Government would not be precipitate
in such an important matter, he informed Bishop Lartigue of Montreal;
and he preferred to play an independent role rather than be associated
with a formal deputation.

> Besides that much information has been obtained since
> last year of the views and designs of the adverse party
> that will enable me to occupy more advantageous ground
> with the Government of England than I could have done
> had I left the Canadas at an earlier period. By going
> alone and appearing in my proper character as advocate
> and agent of the Canadian Clergy and Canadian Church, I
> shall be less suspected of being a party in politics.[38]

The practical shrewdness evident here is an interesting contrast with
the more flamboyant letter to Viscount Sidmouth which was written
largely for effect.

His decision to go to England was warmly supported by the Lower
Canadian hierarchy,[39] and by his old friend James Baby, the Legislative
Councillor, who urged

> The majesty of your presence at Home to enforce your claims,
> at the same time you will have the opportunity of giving

---

[38] Ibid., Macdonell to Lartigue, n.d. (probably early April 1823).

[39] R.A.Q., 1941-42, Correspondence of Jean-Jacques Lartigue,
Lartigue to Plessis, 17 May 1823.

your opinion on the weighty measure of that union which I
continue to believe will prove a source of much displeasure
to these provinces and the Mother Country should it take
place. I own my incapacity to discover the great benefit
so many seem to expect from it.[40]

There were now only details to clear up before Macdonell departed on

his second journey home since he had arrived in Upper Canada twenty

years before. One which must have given him great pleasure was his

election as President of the Highland Society of Canada, in succession

to Maitland who accepted the position of Honourary President.[41] He

took care, before he left, to place himself at the disposal of

Major Hillier, Maitland's closest confidant.

I do not know how to thank you for all the trouble you
have taken on my account, and the warm and friendly
interest you have always taken in my affairs.

I shall expect to leave this in eight or ten days
but will remain for a week in Montreal and from thence
proceed to New York where I shall call on Mr. Moore
for your despatches. It would afford me much pleasure
to have it in my power to execute any command for you
in England or anywhere else.[42]

After a brief visit with Bishop Lartigue in Montreal, Macdonell went on

to New York, warmed by the glowing introductions with which Lord Dalhousie

had furnished him for officials in England.[43] They must have encouraged

---

[40]A.A.T., Macdonell Papers, Baby to Macdonell, n.d. (early 1823?)

[41]P.A.C., McGillivray Papers, Vol. 6, Minutes of the Highland
Society of Canada, 1823.

[42]P.A.C., Upper Canada Sundries, Macdonell to Hillier, 25 April
1823. F.M. Quealey, op. cit., argues that no one had greater influence
with Maitland than his secretary, p. 112.

[43]P.A.C., Dalhousie Papers, Dalhousie to Bathurst; Dalhousie to
Wilmot-Horton, 23 May 1823.

an optimistic hope that he would succeed in gaining both the arrears of
salary and the division of Quebec Diocese, his two cardinal objectives.

IV

Not unnaturally, the Bishop's thoughts turned to the Highlands.
After making his arrival known to the authorities at the Colonial Office,
he set off on a journey to Scotland. Nostalgia, however, did not take
his mind completely from business affairs. Among other visits that he
made, he went to see John Galt, at Eskgrove, near Edinburgh. He was
welcomed by the future novelist and officer of the Canada Land Company
who was at the time acting as agent for Upper Canadians claiming recom-
pense for damages suffered during the 1812 war. Galt recalled a few years
later that Macdonell "gave me all the information I required respecting
the Crown and clergy reserves of the Canadas. From this circumstance the
Canada Company was ultimately formed".[44] The Bishop had brought with him
a copy of the Reports of the Committee on Crown Lands of Canada which he
loaned to Galt.[45] He then proceeded to London to take up his own business
with the Colonial Office, but found the time to act as Galt's emissary to
the Chancellor of the Exchequer.[46] This service done for Galt would pay
susbstantial benefits in the future. The most immediate was a number of

---

[44]John Galt, The Autobiography of John Galt, 2 vols., London, 1833,
I, pp. 294-95.

[45]Galt to Wilmot-Horton, 16 December 1823, in ibid., p. 298. Letter
is in P.A.C., CO42, Vol. 371.

[46]Ibid., p. 297.

shares in the newly formed Canada Company.[47] It was a good omen.

James Baby's opinion that it would require only Macdonell's presence in London to have his request for arrears satisfied appeared to be correct. After recapitulating what must have become a tiresome story by that time, Macdonell was gratified to learn that the Colonial Office accepted his claim for reimbursement almost immediately, and requested the Treasury to pay the sum of ₤3400 in settlement.[48] This last hurdle--the sanction of the Treasury--was overcome by the intervention of Charles Grant, the future Baron Glenelg and Colonial Secretary, and the Bishop's cousin. Macdonell wrote later to "acknowledge the obligation I am under to you, and to assure you that I have not and never can forget the essential service which your friendly interference with the Lords of the Treasury in my behalf in 1824 was to me".[49] The long and frustrating delay was ended. Macdonell triumphantly sent his thanks to Hillier for

> procuring such powerful recommendations from Sir Peregrine
> Maitland to my Lord Bathurst in support of my claims on
> Govert. I have the pleasure to inform you that these
> recommendations have had the desired effect, and I have
> now to return you my most grateful and sincere thanks for
> the trouble you have so kindly taken on my account, and
> to beg you will have the goodness to express to his
> Excellency the Lt. Governor the deep and grateful sense
> I entertain of his great goodness toward me, and to

---

[47] A.A.K., Macdonell Papers, Macdonell to John Fraser, London, 21 December 1824, in which he authorized payment on his stock in the Company.

[48] Ibid., Gordon (Colonial Office) to Treasury, 20 July 1824. A copy of the original was preserved by Macdonell.

[49] P.A.C., C042, Vol. 382, Macdonell to Grant, 27 February 1827.

assure him that it shall be the study of my life to merit
a continuance of his countenance and approbation.[50]

The aftermath could only have appeared to Macdonell as the bitterest

irony. The £3400 was deposited with the merchant house of Maitland,

Garden and Auldjo which had handled the Bishop's business in London

for many years; and was to be transferred to Montreal. Within a few

months the firm failed, before the transfer had taken place. For

several years Macdonell sought restitution, but in the end recovered

only a small portion of the funds.[51]

This blow was still in the future, however, as the Bishop fol-

lowed up his success by seeking an increase in his own salary. His

own standing with the Colonial Office and Maitland's favourable recom-

mendation were probably sufficient justification for Bathurst's quick

response. Additional support, however, came from a curious quarter.

In a letter from John Strachan to the Colonial Office there was an

unsigned testimonial which read in part:

> With the Bishop it is different, he is exposed to expense
> in travelling through the Province, and is a most valuable
> person, and in order to be useful he ought to possess the
> means of supporting his dignity. Should Catholic Emigra-
> tion be continued from Ireland religious instruction may
> justly be considered an expense.[52]

Presumably such expenditure would be justified in order to keep the

---

[50]P.A.C., Upper Canada Sundries, Macdonell to Hillier, 29 September
1824.

[51]A.A.K., Macdonell Papers, 1824-32, passim.

[52]P.A.C., CO42, Vol. 374, Enc. No. 1 in Dr. Strachan's letter
received 1 May 1824.

Catholic Irish loyal and quiet. There is only circumstantial evidence
that Strachan was lending his influence in Macdonell's favour. Relations
between the two were fairly good at the time. Strachan was in London
seeking a charter for his projected King's College, and the two had
occasion to meet as a letter from James Baby indicates. "Our mutual
friend Dr. Strachan is the bearer of this: Having no doubt but you
will see him I refer you to him for news of this place. I suppose he
visits England for some spiritual, as well as temporal views which
time will disclose. I wish him success. He is a deserving man."[53]
If nothing else, the letter reveals a degree of harmony between Strachan
and the leading Catholics of Upper Canada at that point. The enclosure
in the Archdeacon's letter very likely would only confirm Bathurst in
his opinion since he was quite well disposed toward Macdonell. The
Bishop's salary was increased to £400.[54]

With these temporal affairs concluded or in train Macdonell
turned to the other, equally important objective of his visit, the
matter of the erection of a separate Diocese of Upper Canada. Bathurst
had by this time apparently concluded that the creation of suffragan
bishops in British North America had not achieved the result he had
expected, and he was now prepared to recommend that the See of Quebec
be divided. Lord Dalhousie, the Governor General, who had previously

---

[53]A.A.T., Macdonell Papers, Baby to Macdonell, 5 February 1824.

[54]A.A.K., Macdonell Papers, Bathurst to Maitland, 1 August 1825.
The Lt. Governor had sent Macdonell a copy.

urged such a division, was consulted again. He replied immediately that he had "no hesitation in expressing my humble opinion that it is highly desirable to separate the Catholic See of Quebec from that of the Upper Province, and that Mr. Macdonald [sic] is a most fit person to be advanced to that charge".[55]

There were no ecclesiastical barriers to the division, since it had become obvious that both the geographical extent and the increasing Catholic population of British North America made erection of new dioceses inevitable. The Vatican authorities did, however, wish to be assured that such a departure would win the approval of the British government. They were naturally conscious of the fact that in a non-Catholic country the extension of Roman Catholic religious jurisdictions could easily create friction and misunderstanding. Bishop Macdonell was asked to appear before the Sacred Congregation for the Propaganda of the Faith to explain the position of the officials of Great Britain. His formal presentation has been preserved in the archives of the Propaganda.

Macdonell informed the assembled cardinals that Lord Bathurst had told him that as long as he remained subject to the Bishop of Quebec, he could not expect any substantial help from Britain. If with the approval of the Holy See, however, Diocesan Bishops of Upper Canada, New Brunswick and Nova Scotia were made independent of Quebec, then

---

[55]P.A.C., Dalhousie Papers, Vol. 17, Dalhousie to Bathurst, 19 December 1824.

it could be anticipated that England would support them.[56] The reasons

for the official hostility to the Bishop of Quebec were not made explicit

to him, Macdonell explained, but he felt they were twofold:

> 1. It is claimed that the Bishop [of Quebec], without
> consulting the King, and relying on his own counsel,
> has wrested from the Holy See the jurisdiction and
> dignity of an Archbishop. A new title of this kind
> has greatly disturbed not only government officials
> but also the Anglican bishops both in Lower Canada
> and in England.
>
> 2. It is argued, but I think unjustly, that the Arch-
> bishop of Quebec is too involved in secular and
> political affairs which especially in a Frenchman the
> government does not adequately appreciate. For these
> and perhaps for several other reasons, they wish to
> curb the authority and jurisdiction of that Prelate;
> wherefore they would readily permit the creation of
> Diocesan bishops in North America, provided however
> that the Holy See nominate men of proven worth in
> whom they could place confidence.

This is a somewhat pointed, but plausible, interpretation of Bathurst's

change of opinion, and certainly conforms with that of Dalhousie

expressed four years earlier.

Macdonell went on to relate how he acted then as intermediary

between Bathurst and Plessis, and between Bathurst and Dr. Poynter, the

Vicar Apostolic in London. With Plessis' agreement secured, Bathurst

and Poynter then urged him to undertake his journey to Rome and present

the British government's hearty approbation of the scheme for division.

Bathurst recommended the immediate erection of the new dioceses under

---

[56]The Vatican, Archivio della Propaganda Fide, Acta 188, 1825;
Proposals made by Alexander Macdonell, Bishop of Rhesina, pp. 6-10,
original in Latin. This and subsequent references, unless noted, are
from this document.

the jurisdiction of Bishops MacEachern in New Brunswick and Bishop Fraser
in Nova Scotia.[57] With becoming modesty, Macdonell did not urge his
own case for the Bishopric of Upper Canada, even though he was fully
aware that Bathurst had recommended him. "British officials, I do not
deny it, show towards me great trust and kindness, because they have
had more opportunity for friendship and communication with me . . .";
but, he went on, Upper Canada is surely no object of desire, since
"I have had sufficient personal experience of how many labours, toils
and perils had to be endured in undertaking the care of that province".
Macdonell concluded by outlining the spiritual advantages to the church
which would be gained by immediate action in the matter. "No more
propitious occasion offers itself," he ended, "than when the British
regime not only agrees to but solicits such a creation, nay even
promises some assistance."

It had been a very creditable performance. But speed was not
a virtue of the Vatican administration. Macdonell grew restive as he
awaited some reply to the overture he had carried from the Colonial
Office, although he busied himself acting as entree for English visitors
who wished to see the Pope.[58] It must have been with a sense of relief,
and gratifying as well, that he responded to a request to return to

---

[57] It is interesting to note that Bathurst consulted Macdonell on
both these appointments. See P.A.C., CO42, Vol. 374, Macdonell to
Bathurst, 18 December 1824; and A.A.K., Macdonell Papers, Macdonell to
Bathurst, 17 December 1824.

[58] P.A.C., CO42, Vol. 376, Macdonell to Wilmot-Horton, 7 June
1825. See also, R.A.Q., Plessis Correspondence, Bishop Gradwell to
Plessis, 28 August 1825.

London for consultation on the question of Irish emigration. He had
already been forewarned of difficulties with Irish Catholic settlers,
and had been obliged to dismiss a few Irish priests. He had always
been able to vouch for his Scots Catholics, but Irishmen would present
a different problem. But he was sure he knew the solution--firm
guidance in spiritual and secular affairs, but they were inextricably
connected. As he put it in his reply to the Colonial Office ". . . in
order to keep their minds at ease, and give a proper direction to their
ardent and impetuous temper it will be necessary to place a few good
and steady clergymen and schoolmasters among them".[59]

Upon his return to London in August 1825, the Bishop met
several times with Lord Bathurst and other officials of the Colonial
Office. The experiment with assisted emigration from Ireland to Upper
Canada was causing some concern. There had already been riots in the
military settlements in the Bathurst District in April 1824.[60]
Macdonell had, of course, taken an active interest in the progress
of these settlement schemes which were directed by Peter Robinson,
older brother of the Attorney General of the province. If it should
prove that Catholics--even Irish Catholics--were undependable and
troublesome, it would reflect on the reputation of his whole flock.

---

[59] P.A.C., CO42, Vol. 376, Macdonell to Wilmot-Horton, 7 June 1825.
See also A.A.K., Macdonell Papers, Macdonell to Bathurst, 7 June 1825.

[60] See Andrew Hayden, Pioneer Sketches in the District of Bathurst,
(Toronto, 1925), Chapter V; and Mary Agnes Fitzgibbon, A Veteran of 1812,
The Life of James Fitzgibbon, (Toronto, 1894), pp. 147-49; J.K. Johnson,
"Colonel James Fitzgibbon and the Suppression of Irish Riots in Upper
Canada", Ontario History, LVIII, 1966.

In his view, administrative supervision alone would be inadequate.
During the previous year, he had written urgently to Bathurst that he
did not hesitate

> to assert with the utmost confidence that if the Irish
> emigrants be kept under the control and direction of
> proper pastors and teachers their loyalty and grateful
> attachment to the British Government, for the favors
> that have been conferred on them will prove the strongest
> link in the whole chain of connection between this
> Colony and the parent Country.[61]

Macdonell had also made arrangements with Peter Robinson to
be kept informed of conditions in the Irish settlement areas. He
advised Robinson to be sure that a priest accompanied each group that
came out to Upper Canada, since "he would be of the greatest service
to yourself, as he would form a strong link between you and the
people". The priest "could reconcile them to privation and difficulties," he continued hopefully, "and settle their little differences
and help you in keeping and arranging their accounts".[62] In an
attempt to keep in close touch with the Irish, he recommended that
Robinson employ his nephew, Lt. Angus McDonell, as land agent among
the emigrants.[63]

As he discussed the situation with Bathurst in London, however,
it became apparent that another problem had been exercising the
Colonial Secretary. He feared the prospect of the Irish in Upper

---

[61]A.A.K., Macdonell Papers, Macdonell to Bathurst, 19 February
1824.

[62]Ontario Archives (O.A.), J.B. Robinson Papers, Macdonell to
Peter Robinson, 7 January 1825.

[63]Ibid., same to same, 11 January 1825.

Canada establishing contact with the militant Catholic Association of
Daniel O'Connell in Ireland. Macdonell had agreed that any such
liaison would be dangerous. There was an obvious method of preventing
such an event, he shrewdly observed in subsequent letters. Ensure
that the needs of the emigrants are satisfied and they would have no
reason to apply to such a quarter for assistance. If the necessary
churches and schools were provided, Macdonell assured the Colonial
Secretary, discontent would be allayed, and he himself would be responsible for the conduct of the emigrants; ". . . any application
from Upper Canada to the Catholic Association of Ireland for money
would come through me and I pledge my life that I shall neither apply
myself or allow those under my control to apply".[64] The Colonial
Office, as it turned out later, was not unheeding; but Macdonell for
the rest of his life in Upper Canada, would find himself beset with
difficulties within the Irish Catholic community.

It had now been over two years since the Bishop had left
Upper Canada and he was anxious to return. There was little more
he could accomplish in England. His preparations, though, were interrupted by a sad duty. His old friend William McGillivray of the
North West Company lay dying in London. Macdonell was at his bedside

---

[64]A.A.K., Macdonell Papers, Macdonell to Bathurst, 17 December
1824; same to same, n.d. (probably early 1825). It was ironic that
ten years later, as we shall see, he himself sought the intervention
of O'Connell in a matter which concerned him.

the night before his death.[65] His dampened spirit had also to absorb the numbing shock of the potential loss of Ŀ3400 deposited with his bankers. Yet, when he took stock, the journey had been successful. His influence with the Colonial Office stood high; his salary had been increased; and he could look with some hope for further benefits and support for his church in Upper Canada. The great question of the division of the Diocese of Quebec had been resolved to his satisfaction, with the support of Lord Bathurst. As he put it later to his colleague, Bishop MacEachern of New Brunswick, it was "the wish and even anxiety of Earl Bathurst that Upper Canada should be erected into a Diocesan Bishopric, in order to be independent of that of Quebec".[66] As he took leave of Bathurst, then, his resolve was still strong. Despite his sixty-three years, he looked forward to resuming the challenge in British North America. He paid his respects to the Colonial Secretary, and concluded that nothing remains but

> to offer my most grateful thanks to your Lordship for
> your kindness and liberality toward myself, the only
> return that remains in my power to make is to continue
> my exertion to promote Loyalty and submission to the
> laws among His Majesty's Catholic subjects in Upper
> Canada, but your Lordship must be perfectly sensible

---

[65]M.W. Campbell, McGillivray: Lord of the Northwest; Macdonell was, in fact, left a small bequest in McGillivray's will, p. 322. He was very close to the whole family. The Bishop's portrait, done by Sir Martin Archer Shee, President of the Royal Academy, hung in Simon McGillivray's drawing room in Montreal.

[66]Macdonell to MacEachern, 24 January 1826; cited in A.A. Johnson, The Catholic Church in Eastern Nova Scotia, p. 516.

that I cannot be responsible for the good conduct of the
Irish Emigrants until I am supplied with a sufficient
number of respectable clergymen capable of keeping them
under control.[67]

In early November he took ship for New York and then home.

V

The Atlantic crossing provided time for reflection, and with

it Macdonell's natural optimism returned. While his correspondence

at times characterized him as a special pleader, it was because of the

circumstances, in which he found himself. As leader of the Catholics

in Upper Canada, he often felt as a shepherd in a hostile land. But

he never gave in to despondency. It was the successes of his European

mission that assumed importance; the disappointments were allowed to

fade. Upon his arrival in Montreal he went immediately to thank

Lord Dalhousie for his support. The Governor General reported his

arrival to Archibald Maclean, their mutual friend at York, and remarked

that the Bishop "came here this morning and dines with me today in a

family party--he seems in great health and high spirits, having succeeded

at Rome in getting Upper Canada made a Bishopric separate from that of

the Lower Province, and of which he had notice from Rome a few days

ago".[68] In retrospect this had been the high point of the two-year

sojourn in Europe. All that was lacking now was official confirmation

---

[67]A.A.K., Macdonell Papers, Macdonell to Bathurst, 28 October
1825. See also P.A.C., CO42, Vol. 376.

[68]P.A.C., Dalhousie Papers, Vol. 20, Dalhousie to Maclean,
26 April 1826.

from the Colonial Office to the Lieutenant Governor of Upper Canada.

From Montreal, Macdonell went home to Glengarry, but he did
not remain there long. Almost immediately he set out with Sir
Peregrine Maitland for an extended tour of the Ottawa Valley, where
they gave particular attention to the Irish settlements. It presented
the Bishop with the opportunity for long discussions with Maitland
which centred largely upon the growing complexity of the province
which was becoming ever more heterogeneous. Macdonell's most urgent
problem was the influx of the Irish and the necessity of exercising
close supervision over them. Since he felt his own reputation and
influence depended on his ability to establish a degree of control
over the whole Catholic population, the impressions gathered on the
trip pleased him. Upon their return he wrote to Maitland that he
considered it "a most fortunate circumstance that Your Excellency
should have so good an opportunity of witnessing the loyal principles
and good disposition of the Irish Emigrants and of the Catholics in
general through every part of your route".[69] To make his point even
more vigorously, he referred to the somewhat distracted state of
provincial politics, then involved with the contentious alien question,
and the desire of the non-conformist denominations for adequate civil
recognition. In Macdonell's terms, a dangerous situation existed.

The recent occurences that have taken place in the
Legislative Assembly of this Province must convince

---

[69] A.A.K., Macdonell Papers, Macdonell to Maitland, 9 March
1826.

> your Excellency how little confidence can be reposed
> in the loyalty of Sectaries who consider every system
> of Govert and religion subject to be reformed, chopped
> and changed to chime with their own sordid interest or
> capricious humour; nor is it presumptuous to assert that
> the loyalty of the Catholic whose religious principles
> are interwoven with a monarchical form of Government
> and obedience to the authority of superiors hold out
> the strongest pledge for the allegiance of these Colonies
> to the Mother Country.[70]

As usual, Macdonell concluded with a plea for the means to teach and

inculcate this proper obedience; a task made easier, he argued, since

his flock were Catholic.

It is debatable how much effect this sledge-hammer approach

had on Maitland. The Lieutenant Governor recognized the growing

pluralism of Upper Canada. While he was concerned for the position of

the Church of England, he was not as exclusivist as John Strachan.

Nor was he, in general, as antipathetic toward the non-conformists as

Macdonell, as recent research has shown.[71] Yet, Maitland appeared well

disposed toward the Bishop. In a long report to Lord Bathurst--in

which he enclosed Macdonell's letter of March 9, 1826--he expressed

his satisfaction with the loyalty of the Catholics, but at the same

time revealed his anxiety over the persistent requests for more funds

for priests and schoolmasters. "I am much gratified," Maitland wrote,

"by the provision which Dr. McDonnell has obtained from His Majesty's

Government, and which has been abundantly merited by a long, active

---

[70]Ibid.

[71]See F.M. Quealey, op. cit., passim.

and zealous ministry, contributing most materially to the welfare of
the people under his charge, and to the support of the Government, but
I cannot but inquire with some solicitude from what quarter the desired
income is to be obtained."[72] Maitland appeared willing to help, but
claimed that no funds were available. He did suggest the possibility
of the sale of school lands but agreed with Macdonell that the revenue
would be inadequate.

With the prospect of increased support from the local government so dim, the Bishop turned to England, and his recent journey there
again bore fruit. Lord Bathurst approved the annual payment of ₤750
from the proceeds of the Canada Land Company for the maintenance of
Catholic clergy.[73] Macdonell's frequent letters to the Colonial Office
in which he included glowing descriptions of the operation of the
Canada Company may have been influenced by this largesse. John Galt,
in fact, gave to Macdonell a beautiful church site in the newly founded
community of Guelph in the company's tract.[74]

For the remainder of Maitland's administration in the province,
Macdonell had mixed results in his attempts to secure the Lieutenant
Governor's support. When the Bishop petitioned for a further increase

---

[72]P.A.C., CO42, Col. 377, Maitland to Bathurst, 12 June 1826.

[73]A.A.K., Macdonell Papers, Macdonell to Bathurst, 19 February
1827. See also ibid., Macdonell to Panet, 16 December 1826. Panet
succeeded Plessis as Bishop of Quebec on the latter's death in December,
1825.

[74]P.A.C., CO42, Vol. 382, Macdonell to Wilmot-Horton, 5 June 1827.

in his salary, Maitland forwarded the request without a recommendation.[75]
The Bishop was unsuccessful in his endeavour to have the Catholic clergy
incorporated in order to receive and administer property, a project he
had broached to Maitland in 1820 through James Baby, the Inspector
General.[76] The Lieutenant Governor, in this case, appears to have
relied on the advice of John Beverley Robinson, the Attorney General,
who was opposed on the ground that it would probably contribute to the
increase in the Catholic population of Upper Canada. Robinson was,
moreover, quite upset at the increased monetary aid to the Catholics.[77]

On the other hand, Maitland tended to go out of his way to
accommodate Macdonell on matters concerning the rapidly growing Irish
Catholic community. As an example, a riot between Orangemen and Irish
Catholics resulted in prosecutions in 1827. The Orangemen were ac-
quitted and the Catholics convicted. When requested by the Catholics
to intervene on their behalf, Macdonell argued that

> . . . had the Orangemen been found guilty, who according
> to the speech of the Attorney General, and the judge's
> charge to the jury founded on the evidence brought against
> them deserved to be punished I should consider it a whole-
> some lesson to both sides to suffer according to their
> offence, but as the acquittal of the latter party has
> been attributed to the influence of the foreman who is
> said to be an Orangeman on the Petty jury it would afford

---

[75]Ibid., Vol. 381, Maitland to Goderich (who succeeded Bathurst
briefly as Colonial Secretary in 1827), 5 September 1827.

[76]A.A.K., Macdonell Papers, Macdonell to Baby, 11 June 1820;
P.A.C., Upper Canada Sundries, Macdonell to Hillier, 27 November 1826.

[77]P.A.C., CO42, Vol. 383, J.B. Robinson to Hillier, 28 November
1827.

me great pleasure that His Excellency with his usual
goodness would extend his clemency to the miserable
petitioners altho richly deserving the punishment
inflicted on them.[78]

Despite the recommendation of the presiding judge that the Lieutenant

Governor not exercise his prerogative, Maitland did grant clemency to

those convicted.[79] In sum, the relationship between the Lieutenant

Governor and the Bishop can be described as one of careful accommodation.

Maitland would resist Macdonell's pretensions when he considered it

necessary, yet concede enough to keep him solidly in support of the

government. Given Macdonell's predilections, however, he could hardly

turn elsewhere; clearly not to the rising body of dissent in the

province. For his part, the Bishop took help where he could find it.

He was aware of his utility to the local government and exploited it

to the limit. This unflattering description is mitigated by the reali-

zation that both men felt obligated to advance those interests for

which they held themselves responsible. Neither of them appears to

have challenged the political system in which they operated. Macdonell,

especially, played the game as he found it, using whatever leverage he

could command.

During the years of Maitland's administration Macdonell's

relations with Archdeacon John Strachan assumed a pattern that would

---

[78]P.A.C., Upper Canada Sundries, Macdonell to Hillier, 27 September
1827.

[79]Ibid., L.P. Sherwood to Hillier, 1 October 1827; Macdonell to
Hillier, 26 October 1827.

hold until the Bishop's death. As churchmen they remained adversaries, as supporters of the government they cooperated, and on the personal level, the respect in which they held each other grew into friendship. Complex as it may seem, these divisions were severely maintained.

Upon learning of Macdonell's success on his visit to England, Strachan wrote almost petulantly to the Colonial Office suggesting that Macdonell be required to sign a certificate of responsibility for all priests receiving government support. "I deem these checks requisite to secure the peace of the Province and to give the local government that necessary and salutary influence over men who may not always be friendly to our institutions, and of whom some might prove troublesome were there no method of restraining them."[80] Macdonell was just as quick to spring into action when he suspected Strachan of attempting to monopolize permanently the clergy reserves of Upper Canada which were becoming an acute political problem in the late 1820s. The Bishop complained bitterly that Strachan's famous Ecclesiastical Chart had "left the Catholics a perfect blank", and he proposed to send to England a complete census of all the Catholics in the province.[81] Macdonell hoped to enlist William Morris, M.P.P., for Perth, and political spokesman for the Church of Scotland, as an ally. He informed Morris that he had just heard "that the Doctor [Strachan] has obtained permission to dispose of [the reserves] to the exclusive benefit of

---

[80] P.A.C., CO42, Vol. 380, Strachan to Wilmot-Horton, 24 July 1826.

[81] P.A.C., Upper Canada Sundries, Macdonell to Hillier, 26 October 1827.

the Clergy of his adopted Church, probably from some apprehension of being compelled to share them with others".[82] Pouring out his resentment, he even recalled his difficulties with Strachan over the salary problem several years earlier.

> Dr. Strachan and Justice Powel [sic] who in fact
> administered the govert of the province thought
> themselves bound in honour and conscience as sound
> constitutional politicians to check the growth of
> popery by all the means which providence had then
> placed in their power and they shrewdly discovered
> that this might be done as effectually by starving
> to death as by burning to death.[83]

Yet, just as this controversy was developing the personal relations of the two church leaders seemed unaffected. They were consulting on the problem of the Indian missions and Strachan suggested, almost playfully, that Catholic missionaries only led to confusion among the Indians, and the task should be left in the hands of Protestant ministers, since their motives were purer.[84] The following year, an entry in the Archdeacon's Journal, which he intended for publication, described a visit he made to Macdonell's home.

> There is something primitive about the good Bishop
> and his residence. The New Church, which may be
> called a Cathedral, and the schools attached to it
> are according to ancient rule. I have been on the
> best terms with the Bishop ever since he came into
> the Province. His manners are frank, open and en-
> gaging. I spent with him a very pleasant evening

---

[82] A.A.K., Macdonell Papers, Macdonell to Morris, 21 April 1827.

[83] Ibid.

[84] P.A.C., Strachan Papers, Strachan to Macdonell, n.d., 1827.

and often wished that he were not a Roman Catholic;
for his mild deportment and Christian benevolence
would reflect credit on any denomination.[85]

Macdonell, for his part, could show considerable sympathy for Strachan's

position when the latter was attacked by William Lyon Mackenzie; as in

his letter to James Baby, "Our intrepid friend, the Archdeacon is

fiercely and generally assailed by the puritannical round heads of

his native country, but his manly firmness, and undismayed courage

will prove an invulnerable buckler against all their assaults".[86] This

curious ambivalence would persist in all their dealings; but they were,

in fact, natural allies.

In provincial politics, there was, of course, no doubt where

Macdonell's sentiments lay. He was a vigorous supporter of the govern-

ment. At the general election of 1824, when the Bishop had been absent

in England, Duncan Cameron and Alexander Macdonell (Greenfield) had

been returned for Glengarry County. The record of these two members,

especially Cameron, had not been pleasing to the Bishop and his circle

of friends in the eastern end of the province,[87] since they had not

been consistent government supporters. Glengarry politics, however,

were conducted on several levels; Tories against the opponents and

critics of the government, with the former usually prevailing;

---

[85]Ibid., Journal, 30 September 1828. See also A.A.K., Macdonell
Papers, Macdonell to Baby, 4 October 1828, wherein he remarks on Strachan's
visit.

[86]A.A.K., Macdonell Papers, Macdonell to Baby, 7 December 1827.

[87]Ibid., Macdonell to Alexander Macdonell (York), 9 March 1828.

Presbyterians against Catholics within conservative ranks; and the in-
fighting of the large and influential Macdonell clan. The Bishop
came to the conclusion that it would be best to bring in an outsider
who could command general support. After consulting "the Gentlemen
of the County", his choice fell on John Beverley Robinson, the Attorney
General of Upper Canada.

In his overture to Robinson, Bishop Macdonell wrote a remark-
ably frank and revealing letter. After explaining that it had been
the tradition of the County to return a Catholic and a Presbyterian
member, he continued:

> I am myself convinced and so is every elector in the
> County that of all the Candidates that could present
> themselves you are the one that has it in his power
> to do the most good to the County with the least
> trouble to himself, and whatever friendship and attach-
> ment we may possess for you it is but candour to
> acknowledge that the expectation of the good that
> might be derived from your power and influence both
> to individuals and the public has had some weight
> with those who appear warmest in your interest.
> Their land business and aid for the high roads are the
> most important matters, and the matters in which the
> people of this County feel most interested, and I
> should hope that you could promote both these objects
> with little inconvenience to yourself. This opinion
> I have declared in a meeting of the Gentlemen of
> the County, and I think that little pains will be
> necessary to convince the common people of the truth
> of it, and nothing more is required to determine
> their choice in your favour.[88]

In its blunt and unvarnished way, this is what politics was all about;
be solidly in the government camp and have a powerful spokesman at
court. Macdonell went on to suggest that the Catholics of Glengarry

---

[88]Ibid., Macdonell to J.B. Robinson, 27 [December] 1827.

would expect his support in suppressing the Orange Lodges. They would
be willing to take their chances with him on the clergy reserves question;
but, Macdonell allowed, the Presbyterians might react differently.[89]
The Bishop concluded the letter by speculating upon a possible running-
mate for Robinson in the two member constituency, and indicated his
preference for Alexander McMartin, a prominent local Presbyterian who
sat for Glengarry in several Parliaments.[90]

There is no record in the manuscript papers of either Macdonell
or Robinson of the Attorney General's response. In any case, he declined the offer, and stood, as usual, for York Town. The Bishop then
turned to Alexander Macdonell of York as a possible candidate. He
explained to him that "the Presbyterians of Glengarry are quite violent
against the Attorney General, under the impression that he is a mortal
enemy of their church even more so than my friend the Hon. and Venerable
Rev'd Doctor."[91] Macdonell feared that the conservative vote would be
split by a faction fight, and he urged his namesake to come down to
Glengarry. The Presbyterians were busy.

> Colonel Fraser is quite active and on the move night and
> day soliciting votes, he has committed a piece of over-
> sight by declaring [sic] that he will be in over the
> necks of all the McDonells of the County--a declaration

---

[89] Ibid.

[90] Ibid. See also MG 24, C37; Alexander McMartin Papers,
Archibald Connell to McMartin, 11 December 1827, which indicates that
the Bishop's support was not especially welcomed by the Presbyterian
faction.

[91] A.A.K., Macdonell Papers, Macdonell to Alexander Macdonell
(York), 9 March 1828.

that has raised the indignation of many and the hostility
of the whole of our noble and high-minded clan against
him.[92]

To the Bishop's dismay, however, the Catholic conservatives could not

agree on a candidate and Fraser was returned to take his place in an

Assembly with an anti-government majority.[93] Despite their steady

support of the administration, Fraser and McMartin were able to ac-

complish little in the Assembly, although Macdonell seemed well enough

pleased with their efforts.

As the excitement of the election faded, Macdonell was soon

preoccupied with other affairs. Maitland had been Lieutenant Governor

for ten years and would soon leave to take up a new position. Despite

the degree of success the Bishop had achieved in his connection with

government, his private opinion was not one of regret when he heard

the news. As he wrote to his old confidant, James Baby; "it would

appear that we are to lose Sir Peregrine, and to have another governor

in his place. I wish the change may be for the better. I know nothing

---

[92]Ibid. Fraser and the Bishop were well acquainted and, in
future, would be close allies. The latter, however, would have much
preferred one of his clansmen.

[93]For some reason, only one member was returned from Glengarry
in 1828. In every election from 1808 to 1836 the County was represented
by two members except in this election. See Journals of the House of
Assembly of Upper Canada; Wilfred Campbell, "A List of the Members of
the House of Assembly for Upper Canada from 1792, to the Union in 1841",
Royal Society of Canada, Transactions, Third Series, 1910, Section II,
pp. 169-190; and F.H. Armstrong, Handbook of Upper Canadian Chronology
and Territorial Legislation, (London, Ontario, 1967), pp. 69, 84. To
add to the confusion the Canadian Freeman, 7 August 1828 reported
Alexander McMartin returned as the second member for Glengarry; as did
the Brockville Gazette, 22 August 1828.

of Sir John Coleburn [sic]".[94] If the new Lieutenant Governor,

Sir John Colborne, was an unknown quantity to whom Macdonell would

have to accommodate himself, he would also be confronted with an older

problem which was quickly coming to a head. The Bishop, as we have

seen, considered one of his major challenges to be the assimilation

of Irish Catholics into the stable, conservative society of Upper

Canada which he was attempting to mould. A threat to this objective

would be the appearance of someone who could mislead the Irish into

dangerous paths. Such a man now presented himself to Bishop Macdonell

in the person of an Irish priest named William John O'Grady. His

star-crossed career in Upper Canada would shake the Bishop's influence

over his flock, and involve him more deeply in the politics of the

province.

---

[94] A.A.K., Macdonell Papers, Macdonell to Baby, 4 October 1828.

CHAPTER IV

COLBORNE: THE FIRST PHASE

I

When Lieutenant Governor Sir Peregrine Maitland bade farewell
to Upper Canada near the end of 1828, his administration of ten years
appeared to have been successful. The province had experienced a satis-
fying period of growth. Great public works--the Welland and Rideau
Canals--had been undertaken. The wilderness frontier was in retreat,
beaten back by the agency of the Canada Land Company and the pioneering spirit of thousands of new settlers arriving each year. Much of
Upper Canada was taking on the visage of a settled and prospering community, its productive fields dotted here and there with burgeoning
urban centres catering to the needs of agriculture. It was a pleasant
image, but a superficial one.

The growth was real enough, it was the image that was deceptive.
Upper Canada, in 1828, was a society under severe constraints. The
parameters had been drawn by that group which came into positions of
authority and influence immediately after the war with the United
States. Their design was clear, as we have seen, maintain the British
connection and monarchical institutions; establish the Church of
England, as much for its social utility as for its manifestation of

the link with the Mother country; and strive for a society in which those marks of distinction and respectability buttress the whole. Nor did they neglect economic development. Their contribution was permanent, as they fostered that collaboration of government and private capital which became characteristic of the Canadian method of undertaking and completing projects beyond the capacities or willingness of the private sector. But their determination demanded excessive vigilance and control which bred a political system that became increasingly inflexible and unresponsive to the needs and desires of a changing province.

It was inevitable that a reform movement reflecting the growing diversity and pluralism of Upper Canada should arise. That this movement was itself diverse--ranging from the single-minded but cautious objectives of Robert Baldwin to the frantic vagaries of William Lyon Mackenzie--simply demonstrates the increasing complexity of Upper Canada. Like most reform movements, that in the young province tended to oversimplify and seek panaceas. More and more, however, dissent came to focus on the political system which was rooted in the Constitutional Act of 1791 and consolidated during Maitland's administration. It was a disturbing event in Sir Peregrine's last year in office--an election year--to see the Legislative Assembly captured by a majority which rejected many of the assumptions and convictions of the "Family Compact", and clamoured for change. During the next few years they would challenge almost every element of the political structure which the conservative group had bent to their design. The reformers questioned the fitness of a "military person" as Lieutenant Governor;

bitterly assailed the composition and function of the Legislative Council, which seemed--and largely was--indistinguishable from the executive; and deplored the inability of the Assembly to effect remedies. At a lower level, and thus closer to the mass of the inhabitants, there were objections to judges who held office during pleasure rather than good behaviour, the jury system which, it was claimed, was open to manipulation, and especially, to those appointed jacks-of-all-administrative-trades, the sheriffs and magistrates.

There was, as yet, no effective political organization to marshall this discontent; indeed, hardly any coherent means of expressing it. The proliferating newspapers of the time tended to be expressions of the editor's views. They could be roughly divided between those which supported or opposed the government, and official printing contracts were an important determining factor. The electoral process still seemed to revolve very much around the local reputation of the candidates, rather than be contested on broad party programmes or principles. There were also hard, practical issues. The farmers complained, for example, that American agricultural produce could enter the province duty free, and then flow into the British market under preferential terms, while the United States maintained a tariff against the produce of Upper Canada.

As Maitland realized, therefore, the discontent was present even if poorly articulated. But it would be his successor, Sir John Colborne, who would be forced to respond to it. The immediate future would be determined, to an important extent, by the degree to which Colborne's relations with his senior advisors, conservatives all, paralleled that of his predecessor. The 'Compact' was also aware, naturally, that its design and methods were not receiving universal approbation in the province. But its members did not assume the position of a beleagured minority clinging desperately to power and perquisites. They were convinced that the broad outline of their conception of Upper Canada was not unacceptable to a majority of the population of the province. But it was part of their eventual failure that they essayed to defend the whole edifice rather than conceding in detail in order to preserve the essential. Their attitude may have been summed up by John Strachan when he observed unhappily to Maitland, a few years later, that "Sir John [Colborne] from the first sought to be popular at all hazards but having no system he has missed his object".[1]

Bishop Alexander Macdonell, as one of the more prominent conservatives in the province, shared the general apprehension bred by troubled times. After twenty-four years in Upper Canada, he had learned to work within the limits of his circumstances as he understood them. The advent of a new Lieutenant Governor did not upset him unduly. He had coped successfully with that problem on other occasions. But the apparent dissatisfaction of large numbers of people both irritated and disturbed him. He had been disappointed, at times, in his dealings with the government; but it would never occur to him that the system was at fault. Men of small minds and petty motives might frustrate

---

[1] P.A.C., Strachan Papers, Letter Book 2, Strachan to Maitland, 20 April 1833. Italics added.

him in their exercise of authority, but the system of government was
authorized by the King and sanctioned by time. The voices of complaint,
to Macdonell then, were not simply wrong-headed, but wicked and disloyal.

He dreaded the possibility that the contagion might infect the
Irish Catholics, that volatile and rapidly-increasing portion of his
flock. In his endeavour to exercise control over them he sought as
many Irish priests as he was able to attract to the province, being
persuaded that they would have more influence over their fellow countrymen than any others he might send among them. It was for this reason
he accepted the proffered services of Father William John O'Grady, and
thus began the most painful episode in the bishop's career. While the
unpleasantness revealed a harsh side to Macdonell's nature, the provo-
cation was severe. And we are allowed to glimpse the depth of his commitment to his religion and his people, and the profoundly conservative
cast of his deepest convictions. Since the dispute between O'Grady
and his Bishop eventually involved the authorities at York, the struggle
between them threw into relief the relation of Macdonell to the provincial government and to the Colonial Office.

II

Two hundred and sixteen Irish emigrants lately arrived at
St. John, N.B. from Brazil, who previous to their emigration to South America had been induced to expect fine
farms in that fertile country, when the intention of the
Brazilian government had been to make them soldiers, and

which they nobly resisted. Fifteen hundred had sailed
from Rio de Janeiro for Ireland before the vessel that
brought these left the port.[2]

Many of this group landed up in Upper Canada, and among them

a priest, William John O'Grady, who had served as their chaplain on

the voyage. He immediately applied to Bishop Macdonell for employment

in the province and expressed a preference to be located at York.

Macdonell invited him down to Glengarry, and relying on his first,

favourable impression decided to grant his request.[3] This was not

accomplished without difficulty. The Bishop's nephew, Father Angus

Macdonell, had been serving the Catholic community at York, and his

replacement by O'Grady caused some consternation. In reply to strong

criticism from Alexander Macdonell of York, soon to be a Legislative

Councillor, the Bishop reacted rather testily and claimed that

> If I know my own heart I have as warm and sincere a
> regard for my relatives as any man whatever, and if
> my judgement do not mislead me I have given as strong
> proofs of my regard for them as any person ever gave
> under similar circumstances with those in which I
> have been placed. But I trust I love my God better
> than my relatives and whatever shall appear to me
> best calculated to advance the interest of the Catholic
> religion that I shall endeavor to follow regardless

---

[2] Canadian Freeman, 16 October 1828.

[3] A.A.K., Macdonell Papers, Macdonell to Bishop Weld, 26 November
1828. Thomas Weld had been named co-adjutor to Macdonell in 1826 but
never came to Upper Canada. He was detained in England due to family
and health problems. He was appointed a cardinal in January, 1830, and
resided in Rome until his death in 1837. He and Macdonell remained good
friends, and the cardinal was extremely useful to Macdonell in his
relations with the Vatican.

of prejudice or partiality, friendship, relationship or
any other human consideration. It would be my pride as
well as my Glory to see my nephew preside over the church
and congregation of York, but if a clergyman come from
Ireland, or from Russia or from Turkey who would convince
me that he would do more good and advance more the interest
of the Catholic religion and the glory of God than my
nephew he should at once have the preference in spite
of all the ties of flesh and blood.[4]

He was, however, prudent enough to request that his correspondent

should mark O'Grady's behaviour and report his progress. By way of

justification, he concluded the letter with this explanation.

You say that Mr. Baby and Mr. Macdougal and Mrs. Stewart
and Mrs. Boulton and yourself are the only members of
your congregation not Irish. Pray my dear sir is not that
the strongest motive you could point out to me for giving
you Mr. O'Grady for your pastor convinced as I am from
the knowledge I have been able to acquire of the Irish
character than an Irish pastor can best suit an Irish
congregation? At the same time that I have said this
much in favour of Mr. O'Grady I charge you as you will
answer to the Almighty to inform me if you can discover
anything objectionable in his moral or political character.
I made the same request altho not in such strong and
pointed terms in my last letter to Mr. Baby.[5]

For over four years the Bishop was well pleased with his decision.

O'Grady appeared to be conducting an active and zealous ministry in the

provincial capital. Macdonell, in fact, was so impressed that he appointed

O'Grady his Vicar General with jurisdiction over the western portion of

Upper Canada. They exchanged letters frequently, and O'Grady often acted

---

[4]Ibid., Macdonell to Alexander Macdonell, York, 8 December 1828.

[5]Ibid., the letter also appears in part in Edith Firth, (ed.),
The Town of York, 1815-1834, (Toronto, 1966), pp. 192-93. There are
some transcription errors due to Macdonell's somewhat difficult
handwriting.

as intermediary in Macdonell's relations with Sir John Colborne. As
Vicar General he was entrusted by the Bishop with many delicate assign-
ments in maintaining discipline among the scattered clergymen. It
appears now as the purest irony that O'Grady constantly urged Macdonell
to exercise his authority more vigorously, as when he held out little
prospect "of seeing religion prosper, unless your Lordship shall interfere to enforce a more strict discipline".[6]

There were warning signs that O'Grady was not evoking complete
satisfaction among the Catholics of York, especially from the more
prominent members of the congregation. Shortly after his arrival,
Mrs. Irma Boulton complained gently to Macdonell that a priest as
recently arrived as O'Grady should move more slowly in making changes.[7]
More disquieting was the implication in a letter of William Bergin, a
York merchant, who feared O'Grady was acting impetuously in his attempt
to give prayers in the House of Assembly. "Indeed," he commented,
"I fondly hope his sound judgement and prudence will protect him from
becoming the partizan of any party."[8] This was a Reform-dominated
Assembly which had considered having members of various denominations
read the prayers rather than a Church of England clergyman exclusively,
or, alternatively, abolishing the practice altogether. O'Grady may
have made contact this early with William Lyon Mackenzie and the more

---

[6] Ibid., O'Grady to Macdonell, 16 November 1829.

[7] A.A.T., Macdonell Papers, Irma Boulton to Macdonell, 2 March
1829.

[8] Bergin to Macdonell, 16 March 1829, cited in Firth, op. cit.,
p. 194.

advanced Reformers.

Macdonell chose to ignore these criticisms, and appeared unperturbed. It may very well have been that he was prepared to overlook a good deal in O'Grady's case since he relied upon the latter to keep open the channels of communication with Colborne. "We can never be grateful enough to our good Governor", the Bishop wrote, "nor exert ourselves sufficiently to merit his favour and protection: the credit you have acquired with his excellency, and the good account to which you turn your influence with him, and your energy and zeal . . . are benefits for which I offer up my earnest thanks daily to the Almighty."[9] Even when O'Grady became embroiled in a newspaper controversy in 1830 with a member of the Jarvis family who accused the priest of political meddling, Macdonell took no action.[10] It should be noted, however, that from this point on Macdonell had O'Grady's letters to himself copied into his letter-books, a practice the Bishop did not follow with any other members of his clergy except in isolated cases.

Macdonell continued to hold his Vicar General in high regard until the spring of 1832. Then mounting criticism from members of the congregation at York induced him to take action. It is difficult to tell precisely the immediate occasion of the rupture between them. There was general complaint that O'Grady was neglecting his pastoral

---

[9] A.A.K., Macdonell Papers, Macdonell to O'Grady, 26 October 1829.

[10] Ibid., O'Grady to Macdonell, 1 March 1830.

duties, as in the charges of Francis Collins, editor of the Canadian Freeman, who was the leading spokesman of the Irish Catholics.[11] There is also some evidence that O'Grady was carrying on an affair with a lady of the town; a charge he attempted to refute in a letter to Mrs. Irma Boulton.[12] Whatever the specific reason, the Bishop concluded that O'Grady had to be removed from the provincial capital. He did not suspend him at that point, but felt a transfer would suffice. In his official notification to O'Grady he observed, simply, that "seeing you have entirely lost the confidence of a large proportion of the respectable members of your congregation and consequently that your ministry cannot be any longer of use here I find myself under the necessity to remove you . . . to remove you to Prescot [sic] and Brockville".[13] Macdonell hoped, thus, to avoid any unfavourable public comment. O'Grady's refusal to accept the Bishop's order, however, and his denial of Macdonell's authority to remove him turned the whole affair into an exciting public controversy which was carried eventually to Rome and the Colonial Office.

It seemed, initially, that O'Grady was willing, at least, to consider accepting the Bishop's mandate. He claimed that certain expenditures on the church in York should be awarded to him, as a condition of removing to the eastern part of the province. By mutual agreement, Strachan and James Baby were appointed as arbitrators;

---

[11]A.A.T., Macdonell Papers, Collins to Macdonell, 16 January 1832.

[12]Ibid., O'Grady to Mrs. Boulton, 27 June 1832. Mrs. Boulton had passed the letter to Macdonell who was then residing in York.

[13]A.A.K , Macdonell Papers, Macdonell to O'Grady, 9 August 1832.

and matters were apparently settled at a meeting in early October, 1832.[14] According to Strachan, the Bishop would receive O'Grady's resignation, to take effect at the New Year.[15] O'Grady then peremptorily withdrew from the agreement and announced that he was carrying an appeal to Sir John Colborne. He continued to exercise his ministry hoping to persuade his congregation to support him against what he termed the Bishop's arbitrary and illegal attempt to remove him.

With the dispute thus in the open, Macdonell stiffened. It was no longer simply a question of ecclesiastical discipline between a priest and his bishop. This public defiance of his authority threatened to shake the very foundations of the Catholic Church in Upper Canada. Throughout his many years in the province, it had been Macdonell's objective to present the Catholic community as the most loyal and submissive portion of the population. Upon this depended, he was convinced, any hope for progress and tranquility. Now, at the very seat of government he appeared unable to control not only his people, but his clergy. His apprehension deepened at the prospect of the division taking on political overtones, and O'Grady's supporters linked with Mackenzie whose expulsion from the House of Assembly had recently caused a sensation. This was, partly, the reason for his

---

[14]Ibid., O'Grady to Macdonell, 15 November 1832.

[15]A.A.T., Macdonell Papers, Strachan to Macdonell, 18 November 1832.

hesitation in censuring O'Grady. As Macdonell was well aware, the political activities of the Catholics of York were already the subject of
current speculation. He had tried to intervene, himself, that spring
to keep his people firmly in support of the government. A meeting of
the Catholics of the town had been interrupted by Mackenzie and his
followers, much to the Bishop's dismay.[16] A subsequent gathering had
ended in a public spectacle.

> . . . before the leading Catholics, with Rt. Rev. Dr.
> McDonell at their head arrived, Mackenzie and a con-
> temptible mob took possession of the room, although
> notified not to attend, and refused to retire. The
> Bishop and his flock then retired to a large saloon
> in the Bishop's house, where a most numerous meeting
> took place. A series of resolutions approving of the
> upright conduct and liberal views of Sir John Colborne,
> and disapproving of the misrepresentations of Mackenzie's
> faction . . . were proposed and adopted unanimously.[17]

O'Grady's career, therefore, had to be checked. But when he refused
to leave York, and appealed to Colborne, Macdonell determined to suspend
the rebel and, if necessary, to excommunicate him.

O'Grady sent his petition to Colborne early in January, 1833,
and the Lieutenant Governor promptly passed it along to Macdonell. In
a rather tortured argument, based on the transfer of the ecclesiastical
jurisdiction of the King of France to George III at the time of the
conquest, O'Grady claimed that Colborne, as the King's representative,
had the right to intervene in the dispute and block the Bishop's attempt

---

[16]O.A., Macaulay Papers, Envelope 32, Stanton to Macaulay,
14 March 1832.

[17]Canadian Freeman, 15 March 1832. For a much different interpretation, see Mackenzie's Colonial Advocate of same date.

to remove him.[18] While awaiting Colborne's reply, O'Grady continued

to officiate in the Church and refused entry to the Bishop. To Macdonell,

O'Grady's contention that the authority of the Pope had been transferred

to the English Sovereign was simply preposterous. As he explained to

his colleague, Bishop Lartigue of Montreal, Colborne would never respond

to the blandishments of O'Grady to assume the supremacy of the Catholic

Church in Upper Canada. He went on to recount that

> [O'Grady] endeavoured by working upon their material
> feelings to excite the rage and fury of some of the most
> ignorant and worthless of his countrymen as to threaten
> and swear vengeance against me but I do not apprehend
> the least danger from them. . . . Besides that the whole
> of the Respectable members of the Congregation had declined
> going to church when he officiated long before I was com-
> pelled to proceed to extremities against him, and the
> mass of the congregation have entirely abandoned him now,
> notwithstanding that with the aid of a few bullies he
> contrived to get possession of the church and barred it
> against me but he, and they, shall in a few weeks be
> ejected out of it and in the meantime the Governt.
> furnished me with a very decent and capacious building
> for the accommodation of the congregation.[19]

Colborne, meanwhile, instructed his secretary, Colonel Rowan to

seek the advice of the Law Officers, Attorney General H.J. Boulton, and

the Solicitor General, Christopher Hagerman. The former took O'Grady's

petition at face value, and in a very long, historically based opinion

concluded that Colborne had neither the duty nor the discretion to

---

[18]A.A.K., Macdonell Papers, O'Grady's petition dated 4 January
1833.

[19]Ibid., Macdonell to Lartigue, 13 March 1833.

interfere.[20] Hagerman simply dismissed the matter out of hand, since,
as he stated, York was not a regularly established parish within which
the Roman Catholic religion was particularly recognized.[21] This opinion,
however, may have been conditioned by Hagerman's antipathy toward
O'Grady which he expressed shortly thereafter in a letter to the Colonial
Office describing O'Grady as "a priest in the Roman Catholic Church,
who had been suspended in consequence of his highly reprehensible conduct
and charges of grossly immoral character".[22] Hagerman, himself, was
dismissed by the Colonial Office that very month, and he may have suspected O'Grady's connection with Mackenzie being, in some way, implicated.
It was a nice touch, that after Hagerman's re-appointment, O'Grady should
unsuccessfully challenge him in Kingston in the election of 1834. The
Lieutenant Governor, in the event, chose not to intervene, but at O'Grady's
request forwarded the petition to the Colonial Office.

In his accompanying letter, Colborne informed the Colonial
Secretary, Lord Stanley, that "I have not considered it incumbent on
me, after reading the explanation of the Bishop to order a further investigation into the charges".[23] The dispute was reviewed by the Colonial
Office; and two Secretaries, Stanley and his successor Spring-Rice, both

---

[20] P.A.C., Upper Canada Sundries, Boulton to Rowan, 18 February
1833.

[21] Ibid., Hagerman to Rowan, 29 January 1833.

[22] P.A.C., CO42, Vol. 428, Hagerman to Colonial Office, 10 March
1833.

[23] Ibid., Vol. 418, Colborne to Stanley, 17 April 1834.

replied, in terms exceedingly favourable to Macdonell because of his past services, that it was quite unnecessary to carry the matter beyond their support for his authority.[24]

Expecting little success in this quarter, O'Grady took the only other avenue of recourse, and went to Rome to plead his case in the summer of 1833. At the very outset of the controversy, however, Macdonell had written to his friend, Angus McDonald, Rector of the Scots College in Rome, describing his difficulties with his Vicar-General of York.[25] The letter had been passed on to Cardinal Pedicini, Prefect of the Congregation of the Propaganda. Macdonell received a formal letter from Pedicini which fully justified his actions, and rejected O'Grady's pretensions.[26] When the latter arrived in the early autumn of 1833, therefore, the authorities in Rome were already predisposed against him. O'Grady sought the intervention of Cardinal Weld, Macdonell's former co-adjutor.

In a long letter to Macdonell, Weld recounted O'Grady's unsuccessful attempt to bring his case before the Propaganda. Weld had dissuaded him from making a direct appeal to the Pope, and after several

[24] Ibid., Stanley to Colborne, n.d., 1834; see also A.A.K., Macdonell Papers, Spring-Rice to Colborne, 31 August 1834; Colborne had forwarded a copy of this letter to Macdonell as instructed by Spring-Rice.

[25] A.A.K., Macdonell Papers, Macdonell to Angus McDonald, Rome, 20 August 1832.

[26] Ibid., Pedicini to Macdonell, 19 January 1833, original in Latin.

interviews, finally convinced him that his mission was completely futile.
His only hope, Weld had advised him, was a full retraction and submission
to his Bishop. O'Grady took his departure from Rome.[27] A week after
the Bishop received Weld's information, O'Grady re-appeared in York.
He wrote a brief note to Macdonell requesting an interview, apparently
with the hope of re-establishing their former amicable relations. There
was no indication that he was prepared to make the kind of submission
that he must have known Macdonell would demand.[28] The Bishop did not
reply personally, but had his nephew, Angus, inform O'Grady that he
could not receive him until the formal retraction had been made, as
suggested by Cardinal Weld.[29] This seems to have been the last direct
communication between the two men. O'Grady's career in Upper Canada
was not ended, as we shall see, for he then threw himself into politics
as a journalistic ally of Mackenzie.

This distressing affair not only pained Macdonell deeply, but
caused widespread confusion and dismay among the Catholic community of
the province, and the other members of the clergy. Throughout, it had
seemed most important to the Bishop that his authority be maintained.
This was not simply a matter of reacting to a personal affront, although
Macdonell very likely felt considerable embarrassment at having been
taken in by O'Grady. The major implications were two-fold. Macdonell

---

[27] Ibid., Weld to Macdonell, 5 October 1833.

[28] Ibid., O'Grady to Macdonell, 26 December 1833.

[29] Ibid., Angus Macdonell to O'Grady, 27 December 1833.

was adamant that it was necessary to ensure regular ecclesiastical
discipline. In a province such as Upper Canada at that time, where
communications were slow and priests would not be in contact with their
bishop for months on end, the opportunities for improper, or even scandalous, conduct were manifold. In a religiously-fragmented society,
lack of effective control over the inferior clergy could seriously
damage the church's image of unity and piety. Without a submissive
and dutiful clergy, there would be little prospect of the laity exhibit-
ing that loyal and tractable character that Macdonell considered essential in a country where non-Catholics were in the majority, and the
Church of England claimed an established position. To emphasize the
obligations of pastors to which O'Grady's actions posed such an obvious
threat, Macdonell was provoked to issue the first formal pastoral
letter of his episcopate addressed to his clergy. Its intent was
made clear by the titles of the two major sections; "On the Authority
of Bishops", and, "On the Duty of the Pastors of the Church".[30] After
commenting on the circumstances of his appointment, Macdonell addressed
his major charge, that

> . . . all the Priests of the Province are consequently
> subject to us, bound to obey our orders, and follow
> our instructions; and no Priest is to exercise any part
> of the sacred ministry before he be approved of and
> licensed by us.

---

[30]Ibid., the pastoral letter is dated, simply, 1833.

> Every clergyman shall receive from us faculties in
> writing, according to his situation and circumstances,
> and no Clergyman is to exceed those granted to him under
> pain of suspension *ipso facto*.[31]

That this was not simply an exercise in ecclesiastical authoritarianism is made evident by Macdonell's concern for what he considered the second primary difficulty arising from O'Grady's rebellion. The Catholic community of York had been badly divided with both groups launching petitions to the Lieutenant Governor. The public had been treated to the whole spectacle through the newspapers, with Mackenzie's *Colonial Advocate* defending O'Grady, and the *Canadian Freeman*, edited by Francis Collins, and the *Patriot* of Thomas Dalton, supporting the Bishop.[32] Almost immediately, and inevitably, there was a political identification of the two factions. It was precisely this kind of division, of course, that Macdonell feared. He had worked tirelessly for consistency and solidity in Catholic support for the government. Anything less would jeopardize the granting of favors which he deemed necessary for the security and progress of his flock. It was not so much that O'Grady had dabbled in politics that exercised the Bishop, but that it had been on the wrong side. That O'Grady was supported by Mackenzie was evidence enough of wickedness in Macdonell's view.

To denounce O'Grady for political meddling, however, would lay the Bishop open to the same charge. This was his great dilemma.

---

[31] Ibid.

[32] There is almost a week by week account of the controversy in all three papers throughout much of 1833.

O'Grady had to be stopped; that much was clear. But it had to be done
on the ground of a breach of ecclesiastical discipline--thus Macdonell's
accusation of scandalous and immoral conduct, to the exclusion of any
other specific charge against O'Grady. The Bishop was aware that he
ran the risk of being branded a hypocrite. As we have seen, he had
openly taken a hand in opposing Mackenzie in the spring of 1832. Some
of his priests had been distressed at this intervention; and one,
William Fraser, had chided the Bishop for his actions. Realizing his
vulnerability on this score, Macdonell felt compelled to justify himself in a long reply which tells much of how he saw his position in
Upper Canada, and his conception of the leadership required of a Catholic
bishop.

> I agree entirely with you in the general principal [sic]
> that property and politics are not the best foundation
> and auxiliaries of Religion; but when I look back to the
> settlement of this Province, and view the very slow pro-
> gress that Religion made for the twenty years previous
> to my arrival in the country when neither property nor
> politics infered[?] and compare that with its progress
> for the last twenty years, I do not think that the com-
> parison will warrant the assertion that you have made,
> nor bear you out in the conclusion you have drawn. I
> agree with you most decidedly that for a man's own peace
> of mind, and ease of conscience, the less he meddles in
> worldly affairs the better but I contend on the other
> hand that a man without the command of some means or of
> some influence cannot promote the cause of Religion in
> this country except he be gifted with the power of
> working miracles.

But this influence was to be employed quietly, within the framework of
existing institutions. Overt political action should be taken only
when the structure itself was threatened. Thus

> The only instance in which I could be said to interfere
> in politics was last winter, when by their tool Mackenzie

> the Methodists attempted to upset the Government of this
> country and drive or at least overawe the Lieutenant
> Governor. Upon that occasion I must acknowledge to have
> united the Catholics of this town [York] who were at
> that time very much disunited and distracted and their
> union frustrated the views and designs of the rebels
> and preserved the peace of the country. If that inter-
> ference was a crime I am afraid it is a crime that will
> never be forgiven me because I cannot repent of it.[33]

Macdonell's determination to sustain the status quo, and to

suspend O'Grady in the process, may be interpreted as his defense of a

familiar, orderly world from catastrophe. Thus his equation of Methodism

and radicalism derives not from doctrinal difference so much as from

the social and political implications of a non-hierarchical religious

community. Methodism must be resisted because it is levelling, demo-

cratical and Yankee--familiar terms of opprobrium to Macdonell and

other conservatives. His pragmatic acceptance of the role of influence

and property as manifestations of progress reflects his essentially

complacent and static outlook. That he could look back on his twenty-

eight years in Upper Canada and draw a favourable comparison with the

current state of the Catholic religion justified not only his own career,

but the political system itself. His tendency to inflate the political

importance of the Catholics proceeded from his conviction that it was

largely their political utility which earned recognition from the govern-

ment.

The O'Grady affair was thus a watershed in Macdonell's life

---

[33]This, and the preceeding quotation from A.A.K., Macdonell
Papers, Macdonell to Fraser, 13 July 1832.

in Upper Canada. From that point on he would be an open and avowed
partisan of the government, prompting Mackenzie to remark to John
Neilson, later, on "the vagaries of Bishop McDonell travelling through
the colony in a political crusade, with a pension in his pocket and
religion in his mouth".[34] There is no doubting the sincerity, however,
of Macdonell's concern for his people. He felt deeply that their
interests could only be forwarded within the existing milieu, and he
was determined to accord it every measure of support possible. If
this involved him frankly and openly in politics, so be it. In any
case, since the advent of Sir John Colborne as Lieutenant Governor,
Macdonell was coming to assume a more conspicuous, and thus more
vulnerable position in the public life of Upper Canada.

III

Indeed, the new Lieutenant Governor virtually ensured that
Bishop Macdonell would no longer play a private role in the politics
of Upper Canada, quietly exercising his influence to gain the election
of men of sound principles. Colborne apparently decided soon after
his arrival that representation in the public life of the province
should be broadened. This was quite in concert with his initial determination to try and remain above the various factions, and project an
image of official impartiality and concern for the interest of all.

---

[34]Cited in Margaret Fairley (ed.), The Selected Writings of
William Lyon Mackenzie, (Toronto, 1960), p. 347. Mackenzie to
John Neilson, 28 December 1835.

This attitude could be manifested most obviously by widening the membership of the Legislative Council, and thus demonstrating that, as Lieutenant Governor, he did not intend to perpetuate the policy of his predecessor.

After only a few months in office he wrote to Sir George Murray, the Colonial Secretary, indicating several proposed additions to the Council and requesting discretionary authority in the timing of the announcements. The Macdonell clan was well represented. The Lieutenant Governor recommended both Bishop Macdonell, and the latter's old friend and relative, Alexander Macdonell of York, who had sat in the Assembly as member from Glengarry.[35] He did not, at once, reveal his intentions locally, but found other methods of indicating his desire to conciliate as many interests as possible. He gave a valuable lot in York, "worth a thousand pounds", to Macdonell on which to build a school.[36] Of equal importance, was the fact that "[Colborne] has permitted his name to be announced from the altar as the Patron of the Establishment, and to be placed at the head of the subscription list; and declares that he will afford equal protection and support to the different denominations of Religion".[37] In this long, cheerful letter, the advent of Colborne appeared to Macdonell as the dawning of a new and happier day for Upper

---

[35]P.A.C., CO42, Vol. 389, Colborne to Murray, 16 February 1829. Alexander Macdonell (York) had represented Glengarry from 1800-1812, and again from 1820-23. He had also been sheriff of the Home District. His appointment to the Legislative Council came in 1831.

[36]A.A.K., Macdonell Papers, Macdonell to Weld, 29 March 1829.

[37]Ibid.

Canada. A spirit of liberality was abroad and soon the churches would

all be put upon an equal footing. This meant, of course, to him, the

Churches of England, Scotland and Rome. All others were sects. In his

optimism, Macdonell could not resist speculating on the supposed discom-

fiture of his old rival John Strachan, as he concluded his description

of the new Lieutenant Governor's first months in office.

> In fine [Colborne] has completely broken asunder the
> leading strings of his predecessor and appears resolved
> to walk on his own legs. This is truly mortifying and
> most humiliating to a certain Revd. and Honble. little
> great man, who thought himself so well calculated for
> directing the Councils not only of this Province, but
> of the whole British Empire.[38]

Macdonell was quick to offer his services and support to the

new Lieutenant Governor. He concluded his warm letter of welcome by

impressing on Colborne that he always "had the honor and good fortune

of receiving the advice and protection of my superiors"; and assuring

him that "an experience of a long series of years together with an exten-

sive local knowledge of the Country and a personal acquaintance with

every character of any standing in both The Canadas ought to give me an

advantage which few of my fellow subjects in this Province possess".[39]

At the same time, Macdonell attempted to establish as close a contact

with Zachary Mudge, Colborne's secretary, as he had with Hillier during

Maitland's administration.[40] In an action he would later regret, the

---

[38] Ibid.

[39] P.A.C., Upper Canada Sundries, Macdonell to Colborne, 2 April
1829.

[40] P.A.C., MG 24, A 40, Colborne Papers, Vol. 3, Macdonell to
Mudge, 18 May 1829, p. 360.

Bishop gave Mudge power of attorney to draw the salaries of the Catholic clergy, informing him that, "For your trouble I have ordered Mr. O'Grady to leave two and a half per cent in your hands which I regret to be so very trifling".[41] This arrangement, while convenient to Macdonell, could be cast in a very suspicious light, and was later used against him by O'Grady as evidence of corruption.

To Macdonell, however, prospects could not have been better than in those early months after Colborne's arrival. As he wrote to his colleague and friend, Bishop MacEachern, "Sir James Kempt and Sir John Colborne have raised the hopes and spirits of the Catholics of both the Canadas to a high pitch".[42] Kempt, the new Governor-in-Chief, wrote quite confidential letters to the Bishop on the affairs of Lower Canada, and was quite open to him in matters of patronage.[43] Macdonell's optimism, therefore, was not unwarranted. Colborne, for his part, was even more well-disposed toward him than Macdonell was as yet aware. The Lieutenant Governor took up his project of increasing the Legislative Council in earnest. In support of his recommendations, he informed the Colonial Secretary that "Bishop Macdonell, lately nominated by the Pope, Bishop of Regiopolis, I am inclined to think, should be admitted to the Legislative Council. He has great influence in the Eastern part of this Province, and both he and his flock would be pleased with the compliment

---

[41] O.A., _Macdonell Papers_, Vol. 3, Macdonell to Mudge, 8 June 1829, p. 606.

[42] A.A.K., _Macdonell Papers_, Macdonell to MacEachern, 3 April 1829.

[43] _Ibid._, Kempt to Macdonell, 1 April 1829.

paid to him".[44] Macdonell's first hint of Colborne's intention was conveyed to him by O'Grady who claimed the Lieutenant Governor's "mind was made up on this subject. I hope no circumstances will induce you to decline His Excellency's invitation and that you will make up your mind on residing in future at York, where certainly the sphere of Your Lordship's utility must be considerably enlarged".[45] The news must have been a pleasant surprise to Macdonell, who had just returned from a long summer visitation throughout his diocese.

The Bishop soon had the opportunity of conferring at length with Colborne. The Lieutenant Governor met Macdonell after he had returned home, and the two proceeded to Montreal to visit Sir James Kempt. From there, Colborne and Macdonell travelled up the Ottawa River to Bytown and thence down the Rideau canal system to Kingston.[46] It would prove to be a fruitful journey to Macdonell, despite the fatigues, in his future relations with the Lieutenant Governor. Perhaps through modesty, he did not appear overly enthusiastic about entering the Legislative Council. It was, he informed Weld

> . . . an honor I never expected and which I am in doubt
> whether I ought to accept of, considering my time of
> life and the multiplicity of business [sic] with which
> I am overwhelmed. The only consideration that would
> induce me to think of accepting such a situation would
> be the hopes of being able to promote the interests of

---

[44]P.A.C., CO42, Vol. 389, Colborne to Murray, 23 September 1829.

[45]A.A.K., Macdonell Papers, O'Grady to Macdonell, 28 September 1829.

[46]Ibid., Macdonell to Weld, 20 December 1829.

our holy religion more effectually and carrying my
measures through the Provincial Legislature with more
facility and expedition than I could otherwise do.[47]

Despite the apparent reluctance, he would not hesitate when the oppor-

tunity came the following year.

Through his connection with Sir James Kempt, meanwhile, Macdonell

was helping to forward the journalistic career of Thomas Dalton, editor

of The Patriot and Farmer's Monitor, which began publication in Kingston

in 1828. The Bishop intervened with the Governor-in-Chief to aid Dalton

in having some old claims against the government satisfied. In his

letter of thanks, Macdonell commented to Sir James on "the change which

your Excellency's kind reception had wrought on Dalton's feelings and

political sentiments".[48] It is doubtful if the "change" was significant,

for Dalton had become a warm supporter of the government, reversing an

earlier, radical tendency. Indeed, he seemed very much disposed toward

reflecting Macdonell's views. When he informed Dalton of his success

with the Governor-in-Chief, Macdonell observed that

> . . . I read [The Patriot] with great satisfaction and
> feel confident it will do a great deal of good. With-
> out avowing any disposition to cruelty or revenge I must
> acknowledge that I feel highly gratified and delighted
> at the well merited flagellation bestowed by the patriot
> on the soi disant Christian Guardian and at the exposure
> of the vile rhapsody of the hypocritical calumniator.[49]

---

[47] Ibid.

[48] Ibid., Macdonell to Kempt, 12 January 1830. See also R. Card,
"The Daltons and the Patriot", C.H.R., (June, 1935), pp. 176-78.

[49] Ibid., Macdonell to Dalton, 13 January 1830.

Macdonell and Dalton remained good friends, even after the latter transferred his operation to York in 1832, and published it as The Patriot.

The outburst against the Christian Guardian was not untypical
of Macdonell at this time. He was becoming increasingly concerned with
the appeal of the Methodists in Upper Canada, and felt compelled to do
all in his power to thwart their progress. This was especially true
in regard to the Indian missions. He had succeeded in obtaining land
from Colborne to build a church in Penetanguishine, and had also the
Lieutenant Governor's promise of support for a priest-teacher to be
established there. He urged O'Grady, his Vicar General, to "do your
utmost to get the mission of Penetanguishine established with as little
delay as possible, both in order to take advantage of his Excellency's
liberality towards us and to prevent our poor Indians from being deluded
by the Methodists".[50] As we have seen, and will again, it was Macdonell's
habit to discredit the Methodists by identifying them with republicanism
and "democratical principles". The social and political implications
of evangelical religion were as much, if not more, to be feared than
any threat to Christian orthodoxy. This is made quite clear by The
Catholic, edited by Father W.P. Macdonald and approved by the Bishop.
It was begun in Kingston in 1830, and printed by Thomas Dalton. As an
example, it replied to a reflection by William Lyon Mackenzie on the
political activities of Catholics in the province in the following
manner.

---

[50] Ibid., Macdonell to O'Grady, 20 November 1829.

> And why should not Catholics be allowed to vote freely
> with their fellow countrymen of every persuasion against
> the introduction of a set of spies from the camp of the
> Philistines [i.e. American Methodists]; sent hither to
> undermine our loyalty with their outlandish tracts,
> prayers and preachings; and to pilage [sic] besides our
> pockets, under the guise of religion?[51]

Lieutenant Governor Colborne, meanwhile, had finally secured action on his recommendation of Macdonell's appointment to the Legislative Council. The delay had been occasioned by the necessity of having the Colonial Office prepare a document for the House of Commons recommending a broader composition for the Legislative Council to avoid the "heavy influence of judges and officials".[52] At the same time, Sir George Murray, the Colonial Secretary, was assured by the law officers of the Crown that no law prevented the government from recognizing Macdonell's rank, since the Roman Catholic Church was established in Canada.[53] His appointment followed shortly thereafter. The official mandamus was dated 13 September, 1830.[54] If, as Colborne had suggested, the appointment was considered as a compliment to the Catholics of Upper Canada, a much different interpretation was placed on it in Reform circles. The Brockville Recorder and the Christian Guardian, for example, perceived a conservative conspiracy.

---

[51] The Catholic, 8 April 1831.

[52] See P.A.C., CO42, Vol. 389, 24 January 1830, for the document.

[53] Ibid., Vol. ;392, Law Officers to Murray, 17 March 1830.

[54] Ibid., Vol. 391, Colborne to Murray, 17 September 1830; see also P.A.C., Upper Canada Sundries, 13 September 1830.

. . . when even Head and Bishop (as well as the Archdeacon
of York), has procured a seat in the Legislature, there
to turn every political as well as religious question to
their own advantage. If such be the interference of the
Heads of the Church, what may not the inferior clergy do.[55]

Macdonell seems to have been unperturbed by this type of attack.

Indeed, his primary concern at the time was his continual suspicion of

non-Catholic conservatives whom he still suspected of thwarting his

objectives. Perhaps his elevation to the Council recalled the events

of a decade earlier when he had accused the Council, and especially

Strachan, of blocking the salaries authorized by Bathurst. All of this

he recounted to O'Grady when considering the prospects his own appoint-

ment might open. But continued vigilance was imperative, he urged.

The liberality and manly vigour of Sir John Colborne's
mind had kept our enemies at bay since the commencement
of his prosperous administration, but his great kindness
to us is a sufficient cause for stirring the envy and
malice of those who would wish to keep us forever in the
background and I am sure their secret machinations are
in active operation in other matters as well . . . and
I am very certain that if you are not on the alert and
do not proceed with both vigour and prudence, our Penetanguishine mission will fall to the ground, and the
allowance made to the missionary or teacher of the
Huron Indians will be lost.[56]

This harbouring of old suspicions, while perhaps characteristic of

Macdonell, was somewhat unfair. It should have been clear enough to

him that as his own influence with the Lieutenant Governor was on the

increase, that of Strachan was waning. It was apparent to the Archdeacon,

as we have seen; yet he took the trouble, in 1830, to recommend that

---

[55]Brockville Recorder, 12 October 1830.

[56]A.A.K., Macdonell Papers, Macdonell to O'Grady, 1 December 1830.

clergymen of the Church of Scotland and Catholic priests be appointed
trustees of the District Schools, since "they will naturally take a
warmer interest in the prosperity of the schools than others".[57] In
any case, the events of the next few years would resolve their somewhat
equivocal relationship and bring them into permanent alliance, at least
in politics. Whether he wished it so or not Macdonell, like Strachan,
would become a target for the more extreme political dissenters of
Upper Canada.

He must, however, have taken considerable satisfaction, except
in one, glaring instance, from the results of the election of late 1830,
occasioned by the death of George IV. The new Assembly had a majority
of government supporters, reversing the situation of the preceding one.
The Bishop remained at St. Raphael's in Glengarry, throughout the election
period, and the extent of his political activity is difficult to estimate.
In the eastern end of the province, in which Macdonell was primarly interested, there was a Tory sweep. Glengarry returned Alexander McMartin
and Col. Alexander Fraser, the latter now a close friend of the bishop.
In neighbouring Stormont, two staunch Tories, Archibald McLean, who
would become Speaker of the Eleventh Parliament, and Philip VanKougnet
were elected. Donald Macdonald was successful in Prescott and Russell.

But Macdonell was rudely shocked by events at the other end of
the province. The Baby family had been the traditional political leaders
of this district since the creation of Upper Canada. Francis Baby,

---

[57] P.A.C., Strachan Papers, letter - book 2, Strachan to Mudge,
22 May 1830, p. 90.

brother of the Inspector General, had represented the County of Essex

since the election of 1820. He failed of re-election in this two-member

constituency in 1830. The evidence indicates that it was principally

because of the intervention of Macdonell's only two French Canadian

priests, Crevier and Fluet, especially the former, who supported Jean

Baptiste Maçon, one of the successful candidates. It appears that

Macdonell's outraged reaction at their political activity was made the

more intense for its having been cast against the government side. He

wrote to O'Grady that he had

> no words to express my indignation at the disgraceful
> conduct of the two missionaries of the Western district
> towards Francis Baby the most independent, the most
> upright, and I verily believe the most honest member
> that ever sat in the provincial assembly of Upper Canada
> since its first formation, and a Catholic; to oppose
> such a man and lend their baneful influence to support
> a deep designing enemy . . . ! Such conduct appears to
> me not only mischevous [sic] malicious, and disgraceful
> but downright madness.[58]

Macdonell was greatly distressed by the likelihood that Colborne

would be forced to take official notice of the events at Sandwich. He

was even more alarmed that the House of Assembly should become involved,

"1st, Because the mischief already done could not thereby be remedied,

2nd, because a recurrence of a similar evil may easily and effectually

be prevented, and 3rd. because many of the members of the Assembly . . .

would not fail to seize upon such transactions . . . and turn them to

our discredit and disgrace".[59] To the other successful candidate in

---

[58] A.A.K., Macdonell Papers, Macdonell to O'Grady, 1 December 1830.

[59] Ibid.

Essex, William Elliott, with whom Macdonell was apparently on good
terms, he sent his apologies.[60] To Fluet and Crevier he sent stinging
rebukes,[61] and declared his intention of transferring them, although
Macdonell eventually relented. It had been the Bishop's immediate response to suspend Crevier, if necessary, and he so directed O'Grady,
who was to carry out his instructions. It was curious, however, in
view of the later dispute with O'Grady, that Macdonell directed his
Vicar General to consult Colborne first, since "it has always been a
principle of mine from which I would not wish to deviate on this occasion, whenever I found it necessary to resort to an extraordinary
exercise of my spiritual authority to do so with the approbation and
consent of the temporal power".[62] It was quite possible, however, that
he wished simply to demonstrate to Colborne that he would not tolerate
such anti-government activity by any of his clergy. He was well aware
that the election in Essex would probably be protested, and hoped to
avoid a public controversy by preparing the Lieutenant Governor in
advance. If this was his intention, it turned out well. When the inevitable petition arrived, Colborne promptly sent it along to Macdonell,
who replied that

---

[60] Ibid., Macdonell to Elliott, 1 March 1831.

[61] Ibid., Macdonell to Fluet, 18 December 1830. This involved
Macdonell, incidentally, in a dispute with the Lower Canadian bishops,
who claimed jurisdiction over the French Canadian priests. See R.A.Q.,
1935-36, Correspondence of Panet, Panet to Macdonell, 27 July 1831,
p. 186; and ibid., 1942-43, Correspondence of Lartigue, Lartigue to
Panet, 15 March 1831, p. 101.

[62] A.A.K., Macdonell Papers, Macdonell to O'Grady, 25 January 1831.

I feel myself greatly at a loss for words to express my
grateful feelings and sense of your Excellency's great
condescension in transmitting that document to me in
place of laying it before the provincial Assembly. I
shall not fail to apply as far as my authority extends,
an effectual remedy to the evil complained of, and to
adopt measures that may prevent a recurrence of similar
conduct in the future.[63]

Colborne's inclination to defer to Macdonell spared the Bishop

the embarrassment of an Assembly debate on the political activities of

his clergy. It was not really surprising that the Lieutenant Governor

should take this somewhat unusual action, since he appeared disposed to

give considerable encouragement to Macdonell and the Catholics. The

Bishop was even achieving some success, finally, in having Catholics

appointed as local magistrates in areas outside of the Eastern District,

including the town of Kingston.[64] This was a particular concern of

Macdonell who was trying to forward the interests of his old friend

Walter McCuniffe, a Kingston merchant. He pressed his opinion to Colborne

that every days [sic] experience convinces me of the
necessity of putting a few more catholics in the commission of the peace for this town. This would be the
means in a great measure of removing the jealousy and
distrust which at present prevails so generally among
the Catholics of Kingston and might be banished; and
the person who of all others possesses the greatest
sway and influence over his countrymen in this part of
the country is Mr. Walter McCuniffe a respectable
merchant in this town who is in every way qualified to
discharge the duty of a magistrate, and for whose
prudent and correct conduct I would pledge my life.[65]

---

[63] Ibid., Macdonell to Colborne, 2 February 1831.

[64] P.A.C., Upper Canada Sundries, Macdonell to Mudge, 15 December
1830.

[65] Ibid.

To McCuniffe, Macdonell wrote privately that the present magistrates of Kingston were threatening to resign if the appointment should
take place; but he was urging Colborne to proceed, since "it was now
high time to begin clearing out the Egean [sic] stable of that much
injured community".[66] The Bishop's foray into the faction-ridden politics of the Kingston Tories was not immediately successful, but he would
soon return to the attack. His ability to secure Colborne's agreement
on other recommendations for magistrate encouraged him to continue to
advance McCuniffe's name.

Throughout most of 1831, Macdonell was travelling about the
province. He did not go to York for the spring session of the Legislative
Council to which he had been summoned by the Lieutenant-Governor, because
of a severe problem with his legs. He was forced to seek medical help
in Montreal.[67] After a brief convalescence, he undertook an extended
journey through the diocese. Most of the autumn was spent at Sandwich
where he attempted to restore some measure of tranquillity to that parish
which had been so distracted by the events surrounding the election of

---

[66] A.A.K., Macdonell Papers, Macdonell to McCuniffe, 21 January
1831. See also ibid., Macdonell to O'Grady, 26 January 1831. O'Grady
was also trying to influence Colborne's choice. For a detailed study
of Tory factionalism in Kingston, see S.F. Wise, "Tory Factionalism:
Kingston Elections and Upper Canada Politics, 1820-36", Ontario History,
(December, 1965), and "The Rise of Christopher Hagerman", Historic
Kingston, (Vol. 14, 1965).

[67] Ibid., Macdonell to Mudge, 2 February 1831. See also R.A.Q.,
Lartigue Papers, Lartigue to Panet, 19 February 1831.

1830.[68] He did make one brief visit to the Eastern District during the
year, but his permanent residence in Glengarry was at an end. It was
odd in that he had just prevailed upon the Deputy Postmaster General
to establish a post office near his old house at St. Raphael's, "for
the security and despatch of my extensive correspondence". The bishop
was also given the right to appoint the local postmaster.[69] For some
time, Macdonell had been planning to fix his residence at Kingston,
his diocesan seat. Now that he would have to travel to York each year
for sittings of the Legislative Council, he felt that Glengarry was
simply too remote for a man of sixty-nine to carry out his duties. As
it turned out, he would remain in York for much of the next two years
because of the O'Grady affair.

Macdonell arrived in the capital for the session of the Legislative Council in late 1831. His commission was dated 12 October and
he was sworn in 21 November, 1831.[70] He was fully aware of the political advantages of locating in York, but there had always been a
certain reluctance on his part to do so. The summons to the Council,
however, brought him to the centre of political controversy in Upper
Canada; and his ability (and his inclination) to exercise his growing
political influence quietly was at an end. The Bishop's residence in

---

[68]O.A., James Baby Papers, William Hands to Baby, 2 June 1831.
A.A.K., Macdonell Papers, Macdonell to O'Grady, 27 October 1831.

[69]A.A.K., Macdonell Papers, Macdonell to Deputy Postmaster
General, 6 September 1831. See also O.A., Macdonell Papers, same to
same, 19 June 1832, Vol. 7, p. 1003, in which Macdonell confirms he
has moved to York.

[70]Alison Ewart and Julia Jarvis, "The Personnel of the Family
Compact", C.H.R., Vol. 7, 1926, p. 210.

York also altered his relationship with Archdeacon Strachan. Much of the old wariness dissipated, and the two collaborated openly and often. But on at least one occasion, Macdonell's previous habit of making acerbic references to Strachan in private correspondence would be exposed to public view and give the bishop considerable difficulty.

When he took his seat in the Legislative Council, Macdonell began at once to attempt to secure the incorporation of the Catholic clergy of the province to hold land for church purposes. He had long desired this, since he had encountered several difficulties in the past because church property was held through private trustee agreements, which had not always been a satisfactory arrangement. It is interesting to note that on the day the bill came up for second reading the Journal records the fact that Macdonell and Strachan entered the chamber together, late.[71] The following day, third reading was given, and Macdonell wrote happily to W.P. McDonald, his Vicar-general in Kingston, "I have got a charter to incorporate the Catholic clergy of the Diocese through the Legislative Council without a single dissenting voice, but it has not yet got through the House of Assembly. I am in hopes to secure a major-ity there also".[72] His optimism was misplaced, however, as the Assembly would prove much less willing to agree to his wishes. The bill was not refused by the lower House, but it did not come to a vote that session,[73]

---

[71] Upper Canada, Journal of the Legislative Council, 22 December 1831, p. 40.

[72] Ibid., 23 December 1831, p. 42. A.A.T., Macdonell Papers, Macdonell to W.P. McDonald, 27 December 1831.

[73] A.A.K., Macdonell Papers, Macdonell to Cardinal Weld, 20 March 1832.

perhaps because of the distraction of Mackenzie's expulsions.

As we have seen, Bishop Macdonell became openly involved in the conservative reaction to Mackenzie's attacks on the government. In January, 1832, Christopher Hagerman, the Solicitor General, had succeeded in a motion to declare the fiery editor ineligible to sit in the Assembly. Mackenzie's response was to redouble his assault in the Colonial Advocate, and attempt the organization of political unions on the contemporary British model. At this point, Macdonell had intervened to hold the majority of York Catholics aloof. He followed this up in May with a public declaration condemning the possibility of separation from the parent country which, he alleged, was the object of Mackenzie's agitation. This drew the enthusiastic applause of the Orange Lodge which had never been noticeably warm to Macdonell. ". . . the Grand Lodge meeting in June, inserted in their manifesto a statement that they hailed with delight this attitude on the part of the Roman Catholics and their venerable bishop."[74]

For several months, after the summer of 1832, Macdonell was preoccupied with the challenge posed to his authority by O'Grady. His attention to other matters was only sporadic, but he still continued his campaign to secure increased financial support for his church. The possibility of obtaining a share of the clergy reserves had always been an objective of the bishop; not only for the financial benefit it would bring, but as an indication that the Churches of England, Scotland and

---

[74] Cobourg Star, 5 June 1832.

Rome were to be equally preferred in Upper Canada. There is evidence,
however, that he would be willing to accept an alternative. In a letter
to Cardinal Weld, his former co-adjutor, Macdonell suggested that a
portion of the confiscated Jesuit estates of Quebec, "which [have] been
at length given up to the Colonial Government", would be sufficent "to
get the Catholics of this province put upon the same footing with the
Presbyterians with respect to the proceedings of the clergy reserves.
Sir John Colborne", he concluded optimistically, "will do everything
in his power to support my claim".[75] The dispute over the reserves
would, in fact, continue for years.

Macdonell was, however, accurate in his hope that Colborne would
give significant support. The Bishop had often described his difficulty
in raising funds for churches to the Lieutenant Governor. In response,
Colborne urged the Colonial Office to approve an annual grant of £900
to Macdonell for this purpose,[76] which was acceded to with a promptness
that was surprising.[77] When new areas of the province were being opened
up to settlement, the Bishop seemed to have little difficulty in obtaining land for church pruposes. His petitions to Colborne, usually for
200 acres in each case, were almost invariably granted. As he put it,

---

[75]A.A.K., Macdonell Papers, Macdonell to Weld, 20 March 1832.
For a detailed discussion of the clergy reserves issue see Alan Wilson,
The Clergy Reserves of Upper Canada, (Toronto, 1968), esp. pp. 46,
76, 146, 148.

[76]P.A.C., CO42, Vol. 411, Colborne to Stanley, 5 September 1833.

[77]P.A.C., Upper Canada Sundries, Macdonell to Col. Rowan (Successor as Colborne's secretary to Mudge, a suicide), 22 March 1833, in
which Macdonell acknowledges the grant.

"Sir John Colborne has conferred very valuable properties on the church since I have been here [York] and I expect to obtain still more from him".[78] In other matters of patronage, Macdonell continued to advance the claims of individual Catholics such as Archibald McDonald of Alexandria to whom he wrote, "I have given your name to the Lieutenant Governor to be put upon the commission of the Peace which he promised would be done without delay".[79]

His success in this area was confined to decisions which could be made at the executive level, either by Colborne or the Executive Council. The Assembly continued to be much less amenable to his proposals. At the autumn sitting in 1832, Macdonell failed again in his attempt to have the Catholic clergy incorporated, despite the assistance of Solicitor General Christopher Hagerman. After the appointment of John Beverley Robinson as Chief Justice in 1829, Hagerman emerged as the leader of political Toryism in Upper Canada. Yet, even he, in a House with a conservative majority, was not able to sponsor Macdonell's bill successfully. Hagerman confessed his perplexity in trying to explain to the Bishop.

> You have heard I dare say that the bill in which you were
> interested has been rejected by the Assembly. I certainly
> was much surprised at the opposition made to it, especially
> on the part of some members, for whose support I looked
> almost as a matter of course. Mr. Berzy, for instance
> voted against it. . . . Mr. MacNab and Mr. Bidwell also
> opposed the bill--the latter stating that as the Catholics

---

[78] A.A.K., Macdonell Papers, Macdonell to Bell (Penetanguishine), 11 September 1833, which describes the success of his efforts and ibid., Macdonell to Rev. John Larkin, 20 May 1832.

[79] Ibid., Macdonell to McDonald, 30 January 1832.

had on a former occasion refused to be included in a bill passed for the benefit of all the sects, they were not now entitled to any consideration!

I regret the result very much--principally because you were anxious about it. I think you will in the end obtain what you wish.[80]

This is an interesting example of the complexity of Assembly politics. Berczy was a Catholic; and MacNab, a Tory, who was a death-bed convert to Catholicism. There is no obvious reason why they should not follow Hagerman's lead. The action of Bidwell, a leading moderate Reformer, was predictable. What is puzzling is why Hagerman should have felt he could depend on Bidwell's vote. For that matter, it is somewhat surprising that Hagerman and Bishop Macdonell should now be so close. The Solicitor General had been active in Kingston politics for many years. While the evidence is not conclusive, it appears that the Bishop suspected that Hagerman may have been one of those who opposed the appointment of Walter McCuniffe, Macdonell's old friend, as a magistrate in Kingston.[81] Only from 1832 onward is there correspondence between the two indicating such warm collaboration. It may simply be that as conservatives they were moving closer together because of the threat being made explicit by Mackenzie. This, however, would make the actions of MacNab and Berzy even more difficult to explain, although it must be added that the conservatives were a much less cohesive political group than the Moderate Reformers. In any case, Macdonell had to be content,

---

[80] A.A.T., Macdonell Papers, Hagerman to Macdonell, 17 December 1832.

[81] Ibid., same to same, 1 April 1835: although Hagerman did recommend McCuniffe as a commissioner in the Court of Requests, see Wise, "Tory Factionalism . . .", op. cit., p. 223.

for the moment, with Hagerman's optimism that a future attempt to secure the charter of incorporation would be more fruitful.

If Macdonell was disappointed, he could take consolation from the large measure of success he enjoyed when dealing directly with Colborne. The Lieutenant Governor gave equally important support to the Bishop in the distressing dispute with O'Grady which was reaching its peak in the opening months of 1833. At precisely the same time, a letter from the Colonial Secretary was being carried across the Atlantic which would test the mettle of both Bishop and Lieutenant Governor, for William Lyon Mackenzie had also been very busy in the latter months of 1832.

IV

Mackenzie, after being twice expelled from the Assembly and re-elected, was declared ineligible by that House to take his seat. He now decided, in the summer of 1832, to take his case to England, clothed in the righteous armour of a John Wilkes. He beseiged the Colonial Office with endless letters on the distracted state of the people of Upper Canada; presented petitions testifying to their discontent; and urged a radical change in the constitutional framework of the province.[82] The Tories of Upper Canada were not at all surprised at the erratic

---

[82] Mackenzie's letters to the Colonial Office were printed by him in the Colonial Advocate of August and September, 1833. His attacks ranged across the fabric of Upper Canadian life, but only those connected with Bishop Macdonell are considered here.

vehemence of Mackenzie. They were, however, appalled at the fact that the Colonial Secretary apparently gave credence to his fulminations. At the heart of Mackenzie's charges was the apparent inability of the House of Assembly to affect any significant changes in the economic and political life of Upper Canada. The fault, Mackenzie argued, lay with the irresponsible Legislative Council--indistinguishable from the executive--which vetoed all the necessary reforms proposed by the Assembly It had been true that there was much overlapping of membership in the Executive and Legislative Councils. Colborne, as mentioned above, had attempted to correct this by broadening the Legislative Council, but his additional appointments, including Macdonell, left that body with a deeply conservative cast. This was partly a function of the paucity of men of education and talent in the province, who could make some contribution to public life. Colborne, as he well knew, could only work with the available material.

In his strictures on the upper house, Mackenzie included a direct attack on the presence of Macdonell and Strachan in the Council, and went on to denounce, in general any government support to religion. In a letter to Lord Goderich, the Colonial Secretary, he claimed that Colborne had

> admitted that ministers had no business with secular
> affairs, but warmly thanked the catholic bishop (a
> dependent on the government) for getting up a timely?
> political address in his (Sir John's) favour at the
> bishop's own home; which was afterwards carried into
> the church porch on Sunday for the purpose of obtain-
> ing signatures, after the bishop had preached a poli-
> tical sermon to his flock in which I was spoken of

in the harshest terms he could think of, and denounced
even from the altar.[83]

In an interview with Lord Stanley, who succeeded Goderich at the Colonial

Office, Mackenzie used information he had received from O'Grady to accuse

Macdonell of using the government salaries of the Catholic priests to

influence them politically.[84]

The response of Lord Goderich to these, and the many other accusa-

tions laid by Mackenzie, was an extremely long letter to Sir John Colborne,

which became known as the Goderich Memorandum.[85] He discounted most

of Mackenzie's more inflammatory rhetoric, but among the issues he took

up was that of clergymen holding seats in the Legislative Council. "I

have no solicitude", Goderich wrote, "for retaining either the Bishop

or the Archdeacon on the list of Councillors, but am, on the contrary,

rather predisposed to the opinion that by resigning their seats they

would best consult their own personal comfort and the success of their

designs for the Spiritual good of the People".[86]

The response of the Legislative Council was immediate. An Ad-

dress to the King was prepared expressing the indignation of the members

---

[83]P.A.C., CO42, Vol. 414, Mackenzie to Goderich, 3 August 1832.

[84]Colonial Advocate, 5 September 1833.

[85]P.A.C., R.G.7, G1, Vol. 69, Goderich to Colborne, 8 November
1832.

[86]Ibid., the letter was read in the Council 29 January 1833.
See Upper Canada, Journal of the Legislative Council, 1832-33, p. 100
et seq.

at the attempt of the Colonial Secretary to undermine that independence

which gave to the Council its true justification. How could it perform

its function as the balance wheel of the constitution if it were sub-

ject to the direction or influence of officials at home? The Council

particularly expressed its disappointment and regret that in such a com-

munication "elicited by the extraordinary representations alluded to

[Mackenzie], His Lordship has thought it necessary to make express and

particular reference to individual members of the Council, commenting

on the profession to which they belong, . . . and intimating His Lord-

ship's preference that they should resign their seats".[87]   Both

Macdonell and Strachan were present in the Council when the Address

was agreed to unanimously.

The Tory press was much less restrained in its reaction. The

Cobourg Star, in a slashing defense of Strachan and Macdonell, observed

that

> Never perhaps did a minister of the British Cabinet commit
> a more wanton and unprovoked insult than the Colonial
> Secretary here inflicts on them. He honorably admits that
> no charges are brought against them of violation of duty:
> he confesses he has no power to remove, that no considera-
> tion could induce him to degrade them from the seats they
> occupy, and yet he significantly advises them to withdraw,
> Lord Goderich must be aware in wishing such advice to be
> made public it will be imagined that the presence of the
> Bishop and the Archdeacon is not needed in the Council,
> and that he entertains a belief of some misconduct on
> their part; and if so, he will regret his foul outrage
> on private feelings, for an expression of this nature must
> necessarily poison the peace of two most amiable men. If
> every offence to embruted ignorance [Mackenzie's attack]
> is to subject a Legislative Councillor to be bearded by

---

[87]Upper Canada, Journal of the Legislative Council, 1832-33,
2 February 1833, pp. 115-120.

the Colonial Secretary who ever he may be, and subject
to his taunting language, we demand where is their
independence as a Legislative Assembly, where their
power as a conservative body to resist such rash in-
novations of popular phrenzy.[88]

Three days later, the Kingston Chronicle took up the theme, remarking

that "it can be of very little importance to them whether the Colonial

Secretary has any solicitude for their retaining their seats or not,

and of just as little importance whatever opinion he may entertain.

We are inclined to think there is a further motive than what meets the

eye".[89]   So much for the notion that Upper Canadian Tories were colonial-

minded, submissive and attentive to every English direction and example.

Colborne did not allow the opportunity to pass without informing

Goderich of the reaction his letter had provoked.[90]

    Bishop Macdonell was far too discreet to make any public re-

joinder at this time. He did not wish to jeopardize his standing at

the Colonial Office, and Secretaries come and go. But Goderich was

not yet finished. In March, 1833, he ordered the dismissal of Attorney

General Henry John Boulton and the Solicitor General, Christopher

Hagerman.[91]   Boulton determined to go to England immediately to seek

redress, and he visited Macdonell to secure letters of introduction to

---

[88]Cobourg Star, 20 February 1833.

[89]Kingston Chronicle, 23 February 1833.

[90]P.A.C., CO42, Vol. 414, Colborne to Goderich, 23 February
1833, with enclosures.

[91]See Craig, Upper Canada, pp. 214-15 for the violent reaction
of the Tories.

men of influence in government circles. Macdonell could contain himself no longer, and he poured out his classic Tory view of the recent events to Sir James Kempt, the former Governor-in-Chief, whose intervention he sought to aid Boulton.

"In this Province", he began, "there are two parties, the one rank Republican headed by American Methodists and some other dissenters chiefly of American origin, and the other what is called the Constitutional or British party."[92] After a brief resumé of the politics of the 1820s centred upon the alien question, Macdonell claimed that the radicals "succeeded in 1829 [sic] in returning to the Assembly a very large majority of their own creatures, who are so intoxicated with their success, that no measure however anti-British was too extravagant for their adoption". But the people realized their folly and returned a much different House in 1830. Peace and tranquillity prevailed until the harmony was disrupted by Mackenzie, who "had long indulged himself as the Editor of one of the most Scurrilous, Seditious and disgraceful Papers that was ever published in any country". This "Champion of the Methodists" obstructed the House, libelled its members, and forced that body to expel him. This was just what Mackenzie wished, Macdonell wrote: the opportunity "to raise himself from a mere demagogue to be a patriot". The Bishop then digressed to explain how Boulton, "who is a temperate man", tried to afford Mackenzie the opportunity to redeem

_____

[92]A.A.K., Macdonell Papers, Macdonell to Kempt, 5 May 1833. This and subsequent quotations are from this letter.

himself, but to no avail. He was again expelled, and "went a crusading
through the Province preaching and conjuring up imaginary wrongs and
grievances among the People, making them believe that they were oppressed,
enslaved and tyrannised over by the Government". Then "with a mob of
the most worthless and abandoned rabble of this town" tried to overawe
the Lieutenant Governor, but "the Irish Catholics made use of powerful
arguments to make them disperse".

All the excitement passed away when Mackenzie went off to England,
Macdonell explained to Kempt, and "no people in any part of the face of
the Earth feel themselves more comfortable or happy than the inhabitants
of Upper Canada at this moment". Then came the shocking news that
Boulton and Hagerman were to be removed. If this injustice were not
to be remedied, Macdonell warned, it would "so disgust the Loyal and
well disposed as to weaken their confidence in the Government of the
Mother Country".

This impassioned interpretation was, of course, written for
effect in an attempt to persuade Sir James to intercede on behalf of
the dismissed officials. But it is not far off the mark as an indication
of the threat which Bishop Macdonell perceived in Mackenzie's apparent
ability to influence the home government. British North America, to
Macdonell, was a society of allegiance. But in its infant state and
peculiar situation, this allegiance was a fragile link that could be
disrupted not only by the unprincipled ravings of a Mackenzie but, more
seriously, by any appearance of timidity or reluctance by the British
Government in sustaining the present leadership of Upper Canada. Only

the reinstatement of Boulton and Hagerman would be sufficient evidence to put "a stop to a feeling of diffidence and distrust which this step had already occasioned among some of the most sincere friends of the Government, and which I am sorry to understand is likely to diffuse widely through the province".[93] Hagerman was, in fact, reinstated shortly after, and Boulton was appointed Chief Justice of Newfoundland.

V

For Alexander Macdonell, now in his seventy-first year, the bright glow of Colborne's 'prosperous administration' was badly tarnished. The Lieutenant Governor had done his part; indeed his liberality had opened those fairer prospects to the Bishop and his flock. But O'Grady and Mackenzie had churned up menacing clouds, at once painful and dangerous.

O'Grady's actions had a bitter aftermath. Never again would Macdonell give his trust so willingly and fully to an untried man. If his reaction to his Vicar-general of York was severe and, as we shall see it was very much so, it was because his hope in O'Grady had been so deep. For his few remaining years the Bishop's attitude towards his young clergy became more reserved, less familial. He still welcomed new priests into his diocese--he badly needed them--but they would have to prove themselves. His trust would have to be earned. It is a measure of the man, however, that once done his optimism for the spiritual good they might accomplish returned.

---

[93]Ibid. All the intervening quotations are from this letter.

As for William Lyon Mackenzie, Macdonell despised him. He did
not see the future rebel as a political opponent but a wicked influence
seducing the people from their allegiance. Like the reptile in the
Garden, he must be crushed. To contend with him, Macdonell came openly,
almost cheerfully, into the political arena of Upper Canada. This was
a battle he enjoyed. He could see himself--as did many of his more
sentimental memorialists--as the Warrior Bishop defending his flock.

The shock of O'Grady's revolt and Mackenzie's challenge brought
the Bishop closer to Sir John Colborne. Of all the men who held the
vice-regal office during his life in Upper Canada, Colborne was
Macdonell's favourite. There was a warm sympathy between the two men.
The Bishop supported him loyally and eagerly, and not only for the
favours it might mean for himself and his church. He was probably more
successful in this vein with Sir George Arthur. Macdonell frankly ad-
mired Colborne, and after the latter returned to Britain, his friendship for Sir John, if anything, deepened.

CHAPTER V

THE CHALLENGE OF REFORM

I

Throughout most of 1833, Bishop Macdonell remained at York attempting to restore harmony to the affairs of the Catholic congregation of that town. He was forced to take legal action to regain possession of the church from the rapidly dwindling band of O'Grady's supporters. While the delay was frustrating, Macdonell did not wish to be too precipitate in appointing a successor to his suspended vicar-general. The next incumbent at York would have to be selected very carefully if the rupture in the community was to be healed quickly. In the meantime, his own presence for a period would help to ease the tensions generated by the breach. There was the additional benefit, as we have seen, of direct access to Lieutenant Governor Colborne on the various matters with which Macdonell was concerned. For all this, though, the Bishop was anxious to locate permanently in Kingston, his episcopal seat.

He was conscious, also, that he was now very much in the public eye. The dispute with O'Grady, while probably more sensational than dangerous in the long run, would provide excellent grist for the gossip mill of a society as parochial as York. Added to this, Macdonell was now counted among the growing number of Upper Canadians who were featured

142

in the pages of Mackenzie's Colonial Advocate. The notoriety which
resulted from the despatch of Lord Goderich (who became Earl of Ripon
in April, 1833) placed Macdonell in a curious position. He was never
a member of the Tory inner circle; yet his obvious influence with
Colborne, his seat in the Legislative Council and his recent political
activity made him a conspicuous target for the strictures of Mackenzie
and O'Grady, who joined the journalistic wars as editor of The
Correspondent. Bishop Macdonell became, in other words, a symbolic
High Tory.

There is no intention here to exaggerate Macdonell's role in
the politics of Upper Canada; simply to point out that his position
made him peculiarly vulnerable. His rank, his long career and the
publicity which attended it and his determined acceptance of the social
and political structure of the province gave to him a prominence which
inevitably drew the censure of the Reformers. Thus, many years later,
D'Arcy McGee would describe the bishop as "the greatest Tory in Canada".[1]
To the extent that this referred to his public image, it is not inaccurate. It should not, however, be taken to mean that Macdonell was
among the leaders of political Toryism in Upper Canada. For the remaining years of his life, despite his increasingly active participation in
politics, he was essentially a symbolic magnet for the attacks of radical
Reformers.

---

[1] Mirror of Parliament, 8 March 1860, No. 7 and 8, p. 2.

II

Since the elevation of Thomas Weld to the College of Cardinals in 1830, Bishop Macdonell had sought another co-adjutor for the Diocese of Kingston. For over two years he had been unsuccessful, largely because the French Canadian hierarchy had been reluctant to part with any of their men of promise. It had been Macdonell's desire to recruit someone from the Quebec Diocese to avoid the friction and jealousy which he anticipated would result among the Scots and Irish Catholics of Upper Canada by the appointment of a new bishop from the British Isles. After protracted negotiations with the bishops of Quebec, and two disappointments, the choice fell upon Remigius Gaulin who, despite his name was an anglophone by birth. Macdonell then set about the complicated business of securing the approval of Rome and London.

In a letter to Lord Goderich, Colonial Secretary, soliciting his support, Macdonell wrote, that "Succumbing under the weight of seventy years myself, thirty of which I have spent in Upper Canada, in the discharge of painful and fatiguing pastoral duties . . . now quite worn out and enfeebled both in mind and body, I feel most anxious to spend the few remaining days of my life in quiet retirement".[2] His enfeeblement of mind did not cause him to neglect requesting an adequate salary for his co-adjutor; or reminding Goderich that "our loyal and steady attachment to the Government, a principal [sic]

_____

[2]A.A.K., Macdonell Papers, Macdonell to Goderich, 22 March 1833.

interwoven with our Religion entitle us to a participation of the
advantages conferred upon others".[3] This was now clearly evident,
Macdonell concluded, and

> Sir John Colborne will, I am sure, acknowledge the loyalty
> and zeal which the Catholics of this town exhibited last
> year, and the spirited manner in which they frustrated
> the audacious attempts of the Demigogue [sic] Lyon Mackenzie,
> and his rebellious mob, to beard the Government, and
> disturb the peace of the country.[4]

Colborne's support was forthcoming, at least to the extent that he gave
strong endorsement to the appointment of Gaulin.[5] Cardinal Weld smoothed
the way at the Vatican, and Gaulin was consecrated at St. James Cathedral
in Montreal, at the end of October, 1833.[6] Macdonell was greatly con-
soled by thus ensuring that the affairs of the diocese were in capable
hands in the future.

Another event in the religious life of the province in 1833 was
more bizarre. Religious convictions and attachments being what they
were in the early nineteenth century, it was always a matter of some
moment if a well-known individual forsook one religious denomination
and joined a different church. This was even more true if such a public figure
became a Catholic. There was considerable consternation, therefore,
when the Honourable John Elmsley, Legislative Councillor and son of

---

[3] Ibid.

[4] Ibid.

[5] P A C., CO42, Vol. 415, Colborne to Stanley (who succeeded
Goderich in the Colonial Office), 30 September 1833.

[6] R.A.Q., 1943-44, Correspondence of Lartigue, Lartigue to
Macdonell, 27 September 1833, which informed him of the details.

the former chief justice, left the Anglican Church and became a convert
to Catholicism. Elmsley was something of a political lightweight, but
the family was socially prominent; and his conversion was a matter of
much comment.

Apostasy was the proper word for it, in the view of Archdeacon
John Strachan, who made the event the text of a sermon from the pulpit
of St. James in York. He followed this up with a pamphlet on the "Errors
of Romanism". It is very likely that Strachan also had a hand in the
publication, at that time, of an edition of Blanco White's, "Poor Man's
Preservative Against Popery".[7] Macdonell, still residing in York,
took no active part in the controversy, and it does not seem to have
affected the relations of the two clergymen. It almost appears that in
matters of public record concerning their religious affairs, they would
assume a conventionally accepted posture, but not allow it to intrude
on their more vital interests. Macdonell did hope that Elmsley would
become "a pillar to the Catholic Religion in this province"; but there
is no evidence that he interpreted Elmsley's decision as a victory over
Strachan.[8] In a rather curious way, the Bishop and the Archdeacon seemed
then to be in agreement on the most important threats posed to their
province, yet take positions on religious questions that are almost
ritualistic. Perhaps, it may simply have been that their long

---

[7] P.A.C., MG 29, H8, McIntosh Papers, p. 78, which recalls the
affair. There is a very sentimentalized account in Brother Alfred,
"Honourable John Elmsley", Report of the Canadian Catholic Historical
Association, 1936-37. See also Kingston Chronicle, 15 March 1834,
which deplored the pamphlet war.

[8] A.A.K., Macdonell Papers, Macdonell to Elmsley, 15 June 1834.

acquaintance persuaded them that public controversy must no longer be permitted to affect their friendship. As Strachan had remarked wistfully,

> The days we spent together at Cornwall often rise before
> me in affectionate remembrance and tho' many years have
> passed and both of us have risen higher as it is con-
> sidered in rank I doubt whether there has been any in-
> crease either of true enjoyment or happiness.[9]

Advancing age and mutual concern were drawing them closer and would do so even more rapidly in the future.

Macdonell's difficulties during 1833 were increased by an interruption in the pension he had received as a result of his military experience as chaplain. This pension, amounting to £100 annually, had been paid first from the military chest and then by the government of Lower Canada. But a change in the mode of paying salaries to ecclesiastics in the lower province took place and the Bishop was somehow dropped from the list. He was obliged to petition Lord Aylmer, the Governor-in-Chief, to have it restored, praying "that he will not be deprived for the remaining few years of his life being now upwards of seventy, of a salary which he has been receiving for the period of nine and twenty years for acknowledged service".[10] Such was his credit at the Colonial Office that his petition was acted upon almost immediately.

---

[9] A.A.T., Macdonell Papers, Strachan to Macdonell, 24 July 1831.

[10] A.A.K., Macdonell Papers, Macdonell's petition to Aylmer, undated;
see also P.A.C , Upper Canada Sundries, Macdonald to Aylmer, 4 June 1833.

The Colonial Secretary ordered that ₤100 a year be paid to Macdonell out of the casual and territorial revenues of Upper Canada in lieu of the money he had been receiving from the military chest.[11] The money was important to Macdonell in view of the unending demands made upon him to assist in the establishment of churches throughout the province. The interruption had been a major irritation.

As if he did not have problems enough, he was forced also to give his attention to the parish at Sandwich, the affairs of which had not been completely resolved since the schism in the congregation during the election of 1830. The patent deeds for the church, school and burying ground had been issued in trust to members of the Baby family and others. The succeeding trustees had become divided politically, and Macdonell now resolved to have the original arrangement voided. He sought and obtained a bill of incorporation for the catholics of Sandwich which "after the most minute investigation passed the House of Assembly and the Legislative Council".[12] In soliciting Colborne's assent to the bill, Macdonell explained that the Letters Patent had come into the hands of trustees

> whose views and intentions were hostile to the interest
> of the Catholics of Sandwich, and their Religion.

---

[11]A.A.K., Macdonell Papers, Stanley to Colborne, 22 December 1833, copy; and ibid., Macdonell to Aylmer, 20 May 1834, in which he conveys his thanks for Aylmer's support.

[12]P.A.C., Colborne Papers, Vol. 5, Macdonell to Colborne, 10 March 1834, pp. 1109-10.

> The members of Parliament from the Western District
> know perfectly well, and declared in their places in
> the House of Assembly, during the discussion on the Bill
> that those Letters Patent were obtained by a few inter-
> ested individuals without the knowledge of the incumbent
> clergymen, the Church Wardens or the parishioners of
> that place, merely to gratify party feelings, and to
> serve Electioneering purposes.[13]

More important than the local politics involved was the fact that

Macdonell was able to get his bill through the Assembly. His stature

among conservatives probably had been enhanced by the reaction to

Lord Goderich's memorandum, and the attacks upon him by Mackenzie and

O'Grady. But if the Bishop was gratified by the willingness of the

Assembly majority to comply with his wishes, the mood would soon be dis-

pelled. The term of the Assembly elected in 1830 would soon run out;

and the ensuing election would result in a House with a much different

majority.

Perhaps he was growing complacent, but Bishop Macdonell gave

only limited attention to the forthcoming election during the spring of

1834. He was preoccupied with his move to Kingston. The church at York

was recovered from O'Grady and returned to the congregation; and Patrick

MacDonagh installed as the new priest. Macdonell was anxious now to be

away and establish the permanent residence of the Diocesan Bishop of

Kingston. He was not free of O'Grady yet, but as far as Macdonell was

concerned, the rebellious priest was well beyond the pale. Commenting

to Colborne on O'Grady's new career as radical journalist Macdonell

condemned him outright.

---

[13]Ibid.

> This Journal became the vehicle of the most scurrilous
> abuse scandal and detraction against highly respectable
> persons in York--and the most private intercourse of
> families and friends came under the lash of his malignant
> censure;--nor was this all;--he made the Church con-
> secrated to the service of the Almighty, the arena of
> his democratical and demoralizing discourses and col-
> lected by means of handbills and placards the very scum
> and refuse of the population of the Town of York of
> all denominations to listen to him.[14]

This would be the tone of all Macdonell's references to O'Grady from

this point onward.

As the Bishop was tidying up his affairs preparatory to his

departure, 'muddy York' was transformed by legislative enactment into

the City of Toronto. There were many who saw the change as presumption,

if not sheer bumptiousness. Indeed, Macdonell was almost flippant in

recounting the event to Alexander McMartin, one of the members of the

Assembly for Glengarry.

> Yesterday was a day of great importance to the city of
> Toronto. The Election for Aldermen and Councilmen
> having taken place. Among the successful candidates
> are Ambassador MacKenzie, Anabaptist Leslie, Tavern
> Keeper Wright, Coroner Duggan and Doctor Rolph, with
> a number of others of low and obscure character, and
> jaw-breaking names whom I find it difficult to cram
> into this letter. It is the public opinion here that
> your expelled confrere Legislator will be Lord Mayor
> of the City of Toronto.[15]

Despite the style, the distaste for the choice of the Toronto electorate

is evident. It is curious that in this letter Macdonell did not enquire

after McMartin's own election prospects other than to request him to

"send me all the news and the politics of Glengarry". The two got on

---

[14] A.A.K., Macdonell Papers, Macdonell to Colborne, 10 December 1833.

[15] Ibid., Macdonell to McMartin, 28 March 1834.

well enough, although McMartin would never be the Bishop's first choice
as a member for the County.

Macdonell was giving some consideration to the approaching
election, especially in Glengarry. His old friend, Col. Fraser was
stepping down (to be appointed later to the Legislative Council), and a
running mate for McMartin had to be found. The Bishop tried to persuade
Colonel Macdonell of Cornwall, Sheriff of the Eastern District, to come
forward, to block the chances of Colonel Alexander Chisholm (another
of Bishop Macdonell's many cousins). "The general opinion here is,"
he wrote to the Sheriff, "that if you offered yourself in due time a
candidate to represent the County of Glengarry, there would be no doubt
of your succeeding. And the government and every respectable person
in this city have imbibed a despicable opinion of my worthy cousin
Colonel Chisholm's democratical principles."[16] He was unsuccessful,
however, and in a further letter, from Kinston, expressing his regret,
urged the Sheriff to see "that he who comes forward be a person of
common sense and sound principles".[17] In the end, it was another member
of the clan, Donald McDonell, who was chosen to represent the government
interest in the election.[18]

There is no indication that the Bishop took any part in the
election in Kingston, although he would certainly follow it with

---

[16] Ibid., Macdonell to Col. Macdonell, 3 May 1834.

[17] Ibid., same to same, 7 June 1834.

[18] Kingston Chronicle, 27 September 1834, which published a "white
list" of candidates in opposition to Mackenzie's periodic black lists.

considerable interest. It was the first real party contest the town had witnessed. Christopher Hagerman was opposed by none other than William John O'Grady. It should be noted that Hagerman's nomination was seconded by Walter McCuniffe,[19] so Macdonell would be well informed of the progress of the campaign. He must have taken great satisfaction at Hagerman's resounding victory; O'Grady conceded before most of the Tory votes were in. It was one of the few bright spots for conservatives, however, as the Reformers captured control of the Assembly. Not even Glengarry held firm. Donald Macdonell was elected, but not McMartin. Col. Chisholm, the Bishop's radical cousin overturned him. Throughout the Eastern District the trend was the same. In Stormont William Bruce, the Reformer, was returned along with Donald Aeneas Macdonell. Archibald McLean, the Speaker, who had represented Stormont since 1820, decided to stand for Cornwall town in this election, allowing Bruce to win. In Prescott, Alexander Macdonell was successful but died shortly afterward. The representation of the County was then in the hands of John Chesser and Charles Waters, who both supported the Reform party.[20]

The conservative reputation of the District was shattered. It would be a gross exaggeration to suggest that the reason was Bishop Macdonell's absence. The Highlanders were not immune to the general discontent of the time and the blandishments of the better-organized Reform campaign. But the results convinced Macdonell that his inattention may have been partly responsible.

----

[19] Ibid., 4 October 1834; see Wise, op. cit., for the details of the campaign in Kingston.

[20] Upper Canada, Journals of the Legislative Assembly, 1834, passim.

III

The move to Kingston marked a significant change in the life of
Bishop Macdonell. He was now seventy-two years of age; a man of great
bulk, now growing somewhat unwieldy. Most of the day-to-day administrative affairs of the diocese were turned over to his co-adjutor,
Bishop Gaulin. Macdonell's efforts were directed to consolidating the
growth of the Catholic Church which had taken place during his many
years in the province. There was a great need, in his view, for a proper seminary to train priests in the future. He was determined, as
well, to try and secure an adequate permanent revenue for the church,
hopefully from the Clergy Reserves, or some other source in lieu of
what he claimed as the Catholics' rightful share in those Reserves.
Clearly, he saw himself, now, as a patriarchal figure, directing in
broad outline the continued progress of his flock. The old zeal was un-
diminished by age, for he could still respond vigorously when he felt
it necessary. But the descriptive adjectives applied to him now con-
noted age and seniority. It marks the continuity of Upper Canadian
life that young men, whose fame still lay in the years to come were
emerging while Macdonell was yet active. John A. Macdonald, for example,
an enterprising Kingston lawyer, "was elected Secretary of the Celtic
Society and appeared at the annual banquet [1835] presided over by the
aging Bishop Macdonell 'attired in the ancient Celtic garb, a fine
figure of a man'".[21] But this observation on Macdonell's position in

---

[21] J.A. Roy, Kingston: The King's Town, (Toronto, 1952). The
description was taken from a contemporary account.

Kingston society is somewhat deceptive. His advanced age did not handi-
cap his energies, nor did it mellow his disposition when his own reputation or that of his people were involved.

The final attempt of O'Grady and James King, a Toronto lawyer,
to discredit the Bishop at the Colonial Office had been rejected by
Spring-Rice, the Colonial Secretary, as noted previously. Macdonell,
in some pique, complained to William Peter Macdonald, his Vicar-General,
that "the answer of the Secretary of State for the Colonies to O'Grady
and lawyer King's vile, villainous falsehoods had not been announced
from the altar. I feel myself however greatly obliged to the editors
of the public prints for doing me that justice which I had a right to
expect from my friends".[22] Apparently, it was the Bishop's opinion
that Colborne had given the final blow to O'Grady's schemes, and
Macdonell wrote to thank him.

> . . . your Excellency's favourable report must have
> weighed more with the Secretary of State for the Colonies,
> than all the representations that could come from other
> quarters.
>
> The subsequent base conduct of the degraded individual,
> who caused so much trouble to me and to the congregation
> to which he once belonged has developed his real character,
> and evidently proved the necessity imposed on me of dis-
> carding him from the Sacred Ministry, and the impossibility
> of ever compromising with a character so completely desti-
> tute of every moral feeling. It is however hoped that
> his career in mischeif [sic] is at an end.[23]

---

[22] A.A.T., Macdonald Papers, Macdonell to W.P. Macdonald,
25 January 1835.

[23] P.A.C., Upper Canada Sundries, Macdonell to Colborne,
16 February 1835.

If Macdonell felt he was free at last of the machinations of his erstwhile protegé, he was quite aware that other important matters demanded his attention. Throughout his career in Upper Canada, one of the greatest drains on his resources was the need to educate and train young priests. He fervently hoped that some method might be found to endow a seminary. There was a possibility that as the various congregations in the province grew more prosperous they might be able to support completely their resident priests. The government salaries might then be diverted to the erection of a seminary. The Lieutenant Governor did not react very helpfully when Macdonell rather obliquely suggested such a move. "I am of the opinion", he replied, "that His Majesty's Government will approve of any regulations that you think it expedient to adopt in the distribution of the salaries of your Clergy provided that the usual returns and vouchers are transmitted to the Government Office."[24] There was, in fact, little more that Colborne could do. He certainly could not authorize the expenditure of these funds for purposes different from the original intention, support for Catholic clergymen. To Macdonell, a blurred distinction could be made as to what point in a clergyman's career the government support was most vital. He knew, however, that he was logic-chopping. So he began the tedious process of seeking Colonial Office approval for withholding a portion of the salaries and applying it to his projected seminary. There was little alternative, since he could hardly expect any sympathy from the newly-

---

[24]P.A.C., RG7, G16A, Vol. 12, Colborne to Macdonell, private, 17 January 1835.

elected Assembly. He informed Colborne that he had petitioned the Home

government,

> . . . praying that the present Government appropriation
> to Catholic clergymen might be applied to the erection
> of a Seminary and paying teachers under the control and
> superintendence of the Provincial Executive Government
> and the Catholic Bishop of the Province.
>
> I could wish to obtain a charter to enable certain
> persons to hold lands in an incorporate [sic] capacity
> for promoting catholic education, but while a party
> adverse to the improvements of the country possess a
> majority in the house of assembly I cannot indulge the
> smallest hopes of succeeding in that or any other useful
> measure that depends on their humour or caprice.[25]

The only other prospect of securing funds for educational pur-

poses, including his seminary, lay in acquiring a portion of the proceeds

of the Clergy Reserves. There was a slight change in tactics on this

occasion in that Macdonell did not petition for a share as a matter of

right, but as a merited reward for past services, both military and

political, on behalf of himself and his people. It may well have been

that Macdonell had recognized the futility of insisting on parity with

the Church of England. There was also the possibility that he was try-

ing to take advantage of the current political situation in the wake of

the recent election. This was certainly the main theme of his request

for aid for Catholic schools, since that religion "impressed so power-

fully on their minds the sacred obligation of discharging faithfully

and conscientiously the duty which they owe to their God, to their

---

[25]P.A.C., Upper Canada Sundries, Macdonell to Colborne,
16 February 1835.

Country and to their Prince".[26] The alternative, Macdonell observed
darkly, was to see Catholics "imbibe those democratical and irreligious
principles which are universally taught in the Common Schools of this
Province".[27] The clear implication would be the perpetuation of ideas
inimical to the stability of the Province. While Macdonell was unsuccessful in obtaining direct government support for his seminary, he
did live to see it built; and largely as a result of his role in the
election of 1836, and its violent aftermath.

John Strachan, as well, viewed the current House of Assembly,
with distaste. He could expect no assistance from that body in his
renewed assault on the home government for the division of the Anglican
Diocese of Quebec, and his own appointment as bishop. Both Strachan
and Macdonell were being openly attacked by the Assembly, and, as a
consequence, were drawn ever more closely together. In marshalling his
case to present to the Colonial Office, Strachan sought the support of
Macdonell to lend outside strength to his claim. The time was, in fact,
propitious, since the Bishop's cousin, Charles Grant, became Colonial
Secretary in April, 1835, and was elevated to the peerage the following
month as Baron Glenelg. This rather dilatory and indecisive man would
draw little consolation from his feeble attempts to deal with the mounting crisis in British North America.[28] Macdonell, however, took the

---

[26] P.A.C., CO42, Vol. 425, Colborne to Aberdeen, 23 May 1835,
enc. Colborne supported Macdonell's petition which was enclosed.

[27] Ibid.

[28] See Lord Glenelg's Despatches to Sir F.B. Head, London, 1839,
passim.

opportunity to advance Strachan's objective in a letter to his kinsman

which deserves quotation in full.

> However extraordinary or presumptuous it may appear in
> me to offer an advice or even an opinion on the appoint-
> ment of a Protestant Bishop for the Canadas, yet as the
> peace and prosperity of the Province in no small degree
> depends on the cordial understanding and unanimity of
> the Catholic and Protestant [Anglican] population of the
> country, I consider it a duty I owe to the Government of
> my Sovereign, and a debt of gratitude toward your Lord-
> ship to inform Your Lordship that no person seems better
> calculated to preserve unimpaired the good feeling which
> subsists between the two persuasions than the Venerable
> John Strachan D.D., Archdeacon of York.
>
> Dr. Strachan and I have resided upwards of thirty
> years in this Province and have always lived on the most
> intimate and friendly terms ourselves and also fortunately
> succeeded in causing our respective flocks to live in
> the greatest harmony with each other during the whole of
> that time.
>
> The Dr. has been in the Legislative and executive
> Councils for many years, and his talents, knowledge and
> activity have been found to be of essential service to
> the Provincial Government.
>
> I think I may assert without the fear of contradiction
> that he is both respected and beloved by every Loyal Sub-
> ject and every man of worth and respectability in Upper
> Canada, and I might add in conclusion that hardly any
> measure would render Your Lordship's administration more
> popular in this Province than the appointment of
> Dr. Strachan to be Bishop of the Canadas.[29]

This is a rather remarkable letter in many ways, not least for

the fact that Macdonell was willing to take a direct hand in the matter.

More important, however, is the revelation of the ideal nature of Upper

Canadian society which the Bishop and the Archdeacon shared so deeply.

Peace and harmony would prevail throughout the province if the

---

[29] P.A.C., Strachan Papers, Strachan to Glenelg, 27 October 1835, enc.

fraternal amity between the Anglican and Catholic communities was fostered and encouraged. Under the direction of their spiritual leaders, this coalition of the loyal and respectable would ensure the stability and progress of Upper Canada. This rather exaggerated, if not naive, interpretation by Macdonell was partly provoked by the excesses of the current Assembly, but it indicates his elitist conviction that society must be structured and directed by men of sound loyalty and proven talents. It should also be noted that despite the formal hyperbole Macdonell was apparently quite happy to recommend Strachan's elevation to a bishopric.

Strachan was obviously touched, and quickly communicated his thanks to the Bishop.

> I return your letter and would change no part of it except one word which I have marked--it is excellent and comes from the heart. I am making a formal application to Lord Glenelg and your letter will go with the documents and recommendations.
>
> I have further to request that you send back to me the first copy exactly as it is now written that I may keep it as a memorial of our friendship.[30]

They would have great need of each other's friendship and support in the days immediately ahead. William Lyon Mackenzie, comfortably surrounded by the Reform majority in the Assembly, now had his platform from which to launch his attack on the "political priests" of the Legislative Council.

---

[30] A.A.T., Macdonell Papers, Strachan to Macdonell, 24 October 1835.

IV

The House of Assembly, in accordance with Mackenzie's wishes,
set up a select committee on grievances with himself as chairman.
Throughout February and March of 1835, it conducted its investigation
and examined witnesses. O'Grady, who appeared three times before the
committee, supplied Mackenzie officially with ammunition to attack
Bishop Macdonell. It was bad enought that he should violate Macdonell's
confidence, but his evidence was distorted, and on occasion false.[31]
It is, in fact, surprising, considering Mackenzie's usual scattergun
approach, that so much of the committee's time was spent collecting
allegations against Macdonell. But Mackenzie seemed determined; and
the main thrust of his assault on the Bishop focussed on Macdonell's
position as a Legislative Councillor, and the funds he received from
the government for religious purposes.

In order to undermine Macdonell's support among the Tories in
advance, Mackenzie read in the Assembly a confidential letter in which
the Bishop had informed O'Grady about his past disputes with Strachan
and others. It did not have the effect of alienating Macdonell from
other conservatives; but it caused considerable embarrassment to him
to have his old suspicions thus exposed. The Solicitor General,
Christopher Hagerman, reported to the Bishop

---

[31]Upper Canada, The Seventh Report from the Select Committee of the
House of Assembly of Upper Canada on Grievances, W.L. Mackenzie Esq.,
Chairman, Toronto, 1835. O'Grady's testimony may be found on pp. 16-20,
28-42, 58-61. O'Grady introduced as evidence private letters written
by Macdonell when O'Grady was still vicar-general.

. . . a debate in the House of Assembly, in which I greatly
regret to say, your name was mentioned in a manner to give
great pain to your numerous friends. It seems that in 1830
you were in familiar correspondence with a person [O'Grady]
here who has since proved himself to be not only treacherous,
but in the fullest and most emphatic sense of the term--
base and dishonorable. In these letters you speak in terms
of contemptuous disparagement of the late President Smith--
Sir Peregrine Maitland--the present Chief Justice--Dr. Strachan
and several others, who had ever been your friends, and
with whom you were living on terms of intimacy and habits
of social intercourse. These letters, the base individual
alluded to, has placed in the hands of another as worthless
as himself, who has read them in his place in the Assembly.
Disclosures of your private sentiments and opinions of
individuals made in so unjustifiable a manner cannot of
course be taken notice of by the parties named in them--
but we must all never the less regret their appearance.[32]

Bishop Macdonell, having little alternative, lapsed into a mortified

silence. Mackenzie's frontal assault on Toryism, however, virtually

ensured that conservative cohesion would be maintained.

He continued his harassment of Macdonell by provoking an Assembly

request for an accounting of the Bishop's handling of public funds

granted to him. The allegation, based on O'Grady's testimony, was that

Macdonell was guilty of misappropriation.[33] Incensed by this public

challenge, the Bishop forwarded the documents to Colborne; but, he wrote

I disclaim most decidedly any right of the House of
Assembly to call me to account for the munificence of
my Gracious Sovereign to me, and to my people, as a
reward for our acknowledged services to our Country,
and I protest in the strongest possible manner against
a proceeding which has been suggested by a rancorous

---

[32]A.A.T., Macdonell Papers, Hagerman to Macdonell, 9 February 1835.

[33]Seventh Report on Grievances, op. cit., p. 30.

spirit of revenge, and carried on, not with a view to public
good, but with the intention of lacerating my feelings, and
destroying my peace of mind nearly worn out with cares,
troubles and infirmities.[34]

In following his inclination to take high ground in his own defense,

Macdonell acted naturally, and to all appearances, effectively, since

nothing further was heard of the matter. The fact that it was not

followed up after Macdonell presented his accounts, probably indicates

that few of the Reformers especially the moderates, placed much credence

in the testimony of O'Grady, and endorsed the grievance report only

reluctantly.

Mackenzie had greater success in exploiting the much more general

and legitimate antipathy of the Reformers toward the Legislative Council.

One result of the hearings of his grievance committee, was an address

of the House of the Assembly objecting to the unrepresentative character

of the Council. In forwarding the address to the British Government,

Sir John Colborne voiced the complaint of almost every Lieutenant Governor

of Upper Canada. In a developing province ". . . your Lordship must be

fully aware of the difficulty of selecting persons qualified for their

intelligence, property and station for seats in the Council".[35] With

these criteria, Colborne was obviously correct. His expansion of the

membership of the Council in his first years in office was simply a matter

of degree rather than kind. Thus "Bishop McDonell was recommended under

---

[34]P.A.C., Upper Canada Sundries, Macdonell to Colborne, 12 March
1835.

[35]P.A.C., CO42, Vol. 425, Colborne to the Earl of Aberdeen,
15 May 1835.

the persuasion that his appointment would be well received by the settlers
of the Roman Catholic Church and that his services and exertions entitled
him to that mark of confidence".[36] It is not surprising that Colborne
felt obliged to defend his choice of Macdonell; but it is worth noting
that Macdonell's "services and exertions", which justified his appointment, were viewed in an entirely different light by the Reformers. As
we shall see, Mackenzie would soon shift his attack from the general to
the specific and demand the removal of Macdonell (and Strachan) from the
Council.

The Bishop, meanwhile, considered Mackenzie's open hostility as
sufficient evidence of his own value to the government. The more he was
criticized as a bulwark of the existing order, the greater would be his
influence. This is apparent even in routine patronage matters. In
introducing "Mr. Macdonald, brother in law to Sir Arch. Campbell Lt.
Governor of New Brunswick", Macdonell recommends him as a staunch opponent
of the insidious seductions of Mackenzie.[37] But the rapport between
the Bishop and the Lieutenant Governor, and upon which Macdonell had
successfully relied, was not to serve him much longer.

The Colonial Office, unaware that the Seventh Grievance Report
was not a true reflection of popular (or even Reform) opinion, was
alarmed at this apparent deterioration of the affairs of Upper Canada.
Glenelg grew exasperated at Colborne's calm insistence that no serious

---

[36]Ibid.

[37]P.A.C., Upper Canada Sundries, Macdonell to Rowan, 8 October 1835.

dissent existed in the province and decided to relieve the Lieutenant
Governor, and replace him with Sir Francis Bond Head.[38] Once again,
Macdonell would have to make the adjustment to a new incumbent of the
vice-regal office; more painfully on this occasion because of his
great affection and admiration for Colborne.

Macdonell suspected that Glenelg, his cousin, may have misinter-
preted the situation in British North America, and especially, in Upper
Canada. Shortly before Colborne's departure the Bishop wrote a long
letter to Glenelg, "under the impression that information from the
Canada's at the present juncture will not be unacceptable to your Lordship".[39] He began by remarking on the contentedness of the French Canadians;
and then castigated Papineau, and condemned his attempts to subvert them.
His opinion of the tribune of Lower Canada had undergone a substantial
transformation since he had warmly supported Papineau in his objections
to the projected union of 1822. "From my own personal acquaintance with
this Gentleman," Macdonell now opined, "I may assert without the fear
of contradiction that his ambition is boundless, that every concession
that is made to him only makes him bolder--and more insolent in his
demands." The Bishop went on to charge that Papineau's aim was "not
only to sever the Canadians from the British Empire but to extinguish

[38]For details of the change, cf. Craig, op. cit., p. 224. Colborne
retained his position as Commander of the Forces throughout the rebellion.
He served as administrator of the government before and after Durham's
term, and left British North America in 1839.

[39]P.A.C., CO42, Vol. 428, Macdonell to Glenelg, 20 December 1835.
The following passage is drawn from this letter.

every British feeling and to drive out of Lower Canada every Loyal

Subject of British origin".

But Macdonell's real concern was to counteract the impression

of Upper Canada held by Glenelg, and manifested in the recall of Sir

John Colborne. The Colonial Secretary must be given an accurate assess-

ment of the real villains of Upper Canadian politics.

> On the opening of the British Commission at Quebec last
> month Mr. Papineau invited to his Councils the two greatest
> Radicals and disturbers of the peace of this Province,
> William Lyon McKenzie [sic] and William John O'Grady an
> appostate Irish priest, a most abandoned and immoral
> character. The former had been a soap boiler in Dundee
> in Scotland, but having failed in business he emigrated
> to this province and commenced a fraudulent trade in
> politics. He began his career by establishing a violent
> and infamous News Paper in Toronto under the appelation of
> Colonial Advocate and to diffuse through this vehicle of
> Scandal the most infamous libels on the Provincial
> Government.
>
> Mr. O'Grady after being expelled from the Catholic
> Church on account of immoral conduct and quarreling with
> Government thought the shortest road to notoriety was by
> establishing also a Democratical Paper which in scurility
> and abuse against the Government exceeded if possible
> McKenzie's Colonial Advocate.

With the leading players of Upper Canada's political drama thus

characterized, Macdonell then described Mackenzie's tactics of fomenting

dissent through the preparation of fraudulent petitions with thousands

of forged signatures. The truth was, according to the Bishop, that

their activities rendered both of them, "contemptible and despised in

the eyes of every person in this Province who has the least title to

respectability or character". Macdonell concluded with the hope that

should these "few traits of the turbulent characters and disturbers of

the peace and happiness of these Provinces prove useful to your Lordship

I would think myself fortunate in contributing my mite to the welfare
of my Country".[40] It is difficult to judge how influential Macdonell's
opinions were on the Colonial Secretary, but Glenelg seemed well
disposed toward the Bishop when the latter was attacked directly by the
Assembly a few months later.

The House had begun an investigation into the affairs of the
Canada Company. Since Macdonell received an annual payment from the
funds which the company turned over to the government, he was requested
to supply a detailed accounting of the money and its distribution.
Macdonell simply refused.

> . . . as this appropriation is from the proceeds of The
> Canada Company and no ways under the control of the
> Provincial Parliament I consider myself responsible to
> the Colonial Minister alone and by no means to the House
> of Assembly to call me to account in that business.[41]

The attitude of the Reformers in the House toward Macdonell would hardly
be mollified by this peremptory response. Their mood, in any case, was
one of bitter frustration when they learned that Sir John Colborne, in
one of his last official acts, had authorized the creation of fifty-seven
rectories for the Church of England. Part of their reaction was an
address to Sir Francis Bond Head, explicitly demanding the resignation
of Strachan and Macdonell from the Legislative Council. The Assembly

> . . . had the mortification to see the Bishop of Regiopolis
> and the Archdeacon of York neglecting their high and
> spiritual functions, and care of souls, and clinging to

---

[40]Ibid. The intervening citations are from the same document.

[41]P.A.C., Upper Canada Sundries, Macdonell to Rowan, 23 January
1836.

their seats in the Legislative Council, and devoting their
time and talents to political strife and secular measures,
in direct opposition, and contrary to the express desire
and pleasure of His Majesty, as set forth in the despatch
of Earl Ripon.[42]

Strachan and Macdonell reacted in concert. In reply to the
Bishop's inquiry about the attitude of Head, Strachan remarked

> . . . that nothing could be more courteous than Sir
> Francis' manner in probing this communication but
> evidently with the view of inducing me to withdraw from
> the Legislative Council. This I respectfully but firmly
> decline. I am not to be driven by wicked clamour and
> persecution from a station conferred upon me by the King
> as a distinguished mark of honour. I thought it proper
> to insert the following passage in my reply to the
> Lieutenant Governor which I hope will meet with your
> approbation.

> 'This direct charge is made with incredible disregard
> of justice against the Roman Catholic Bishop of Regiopolis
> as well as myself. The Venerable Bishop alluded to
> residing in a part of the Province nearly two hundred
> miles distant from the seat of the Legislature has not
> been within the wall of the Legislative Council during this
> session or the last and it would I imagine perplex the
> House of Assembly to specify a single instance during his
> rare and occasional attendance in which he has been found
> engaged in political strife or actively concerned in any
> secular measure.'

> We have nothing here to speak of but political strife
> fomented by the weakness of the Home Government nor is
> there any good in prospect--for it appears to me that
> we shall in a very short time have no other Government
> than the House of Assembly.[43]

---

[42] A.A.K., Macdonell Papers, Joseph (Secretary to Head) to Macdonell
17 February 1836. Joseph requested Macdonell's comments on the address,
which he enclosed, for the Lieutenant-Governor. The address was published
in the Kingston Chronicle, 20 February 1836.

[43] A.A.T., Macdonell Papers, Strachan to Macdonell, 26 February
1836. See also P.A.C., CO42, Vol. 429, Strachan to Joseph, 22 February
1836, for the full text of Strachan's rejoinder. A search of The Journal
of the Legislative Council indicates that after 1833, Macdonell never
took his seat.

Macdonell generally followed Strachan's example in his own reply to the Assembly's call for his resignation. He informed Head that he doubted if "Lord Glenelg who knows something of me would expect that I should shew so much imbecility in my latter days, as to relinquish a mark of honour conferred upon me by my Sovereign to gratify the vindictive malice of a few unprincipled radicals who made a fraudulent trade of politics under the delusive pretext of patriotism".[44] It is obvious in the letter that Macdonell sees no merit in the Reform position that the Legislative Council is a serious impediment to the legislative expression of the wishes of the people. Indeed, he viewed the Assembly address as evidence of the hold Mackenzie (and indirectly O'Grady) had been able to establish over the House. By putting the issue on a personal level he could inform the Lieutenant Governor that he felt "very little affected by the malicious calumnies of two notorious slanderers".[45] Macdonell reciprocated the Archdeacon's gesture of support by claiming that "I never saw [Strachan] engaged in any political discussion of any kind and never heard of his being engaged in political strife, but of his universal attention to his pastoral functions and his Charity to the Poor and indigent of his own and other persuasions".[46]

The semantics of Macdonell and Strachan in this exchange are interesting. It becomes quite evident that 'politics' and 'political strife' are activities engaged in only by those who opposed the status quo.

---

[44] A.A.K., Macdonell Papers, Macdonell to Joseph, 7 March 1836.

[45] Ibid.

[46] Ibid.

Support for the government was never 'politics', but the natural manifestation of that allegiance demanded of all loyal subjects. To oppose,
in their lexicon, is to subvert. They saw no hypocrisy, either, in
regarding seats in the Council as a 'distinguished mark of honour'.
They knew full well that such appointments were not made in a vacuum;
that they had to be recommended by someone, and on specific criteria.
Talent and ability were not enough, or such a man as Marshall Spring
Bidwell, the moderate Reformer, would have been a prime candidate.
Positions such as Council seats were designed to buttress a total view
of society. They were 'marks of honour', surely; but they expressed
that desirable gradation which was the cement of society. To surrender
such a position would concede the point of those who sought to overturn
the structure.

The Colonial Secretary seemed quite satisfied with the reply
of Macdonell. He instructed Head to assure

> Dr. McDonell that I am fully sensible to the high testimony
> which is borne to his services and character by the cor-
> respondence recorded in the Archives of this office. It
> required no further evidence to convince me that in
> whatever course he might adopt he would be guided solely
> by a conscientious feeling of duty to himself and the
> public.[47]

By the time Glenelg's assurance arrived in Upper Canada, however, the
whole affair had become academic. The Reform majority in the Assembly,
frustrated in their endeavours to give effect to their objectives finally
decided to stop the supplies in April, 1836. The reply of the Lieutenant

---

[47]P.A.C., CO42, Vol. 436, Glenelg to Head, 11 June 1836.

Governor was to prorogue the session and withhold his assent to money
bills already passed. The following month he dissolved the legislature
and precipitated the most noisy and exciting election in the history
of the province.

The immediate response of Bishop Macdonell was to send Sir Francis
a public letter of support for his actions, and a plea for determined
opposition to the radicals.[48] In the campaign, Macdonell gave most of
his attention to the Eastern District, where he felt his exertions would
have the most effect. The Highlanders must redeem their foolishness of
1834. It would prove to be fertile ground. The terms of the election
were set by the Lieutenant Governor who took the field himself. All the
issues were over-simplified into one burning question--defense of the
constitution and the British connection against a disloyal faction.
This provocative rhetoric resulted in one of the strangest coalitions
in Upper Canadian politics, an alliance between the Orange Order and the
Catholics of the province under the leadership of Bishop Macdonell.

Indeed, the tide in the Eastern District had begun to turn even
before the legislature had been dissolved. Ogle Gowan, who was assuming the leadership of Orangeism in Upper Canada, informed his brother,
that

> A great reaction in the public mind is now taking place
> in this part of the country and if there was a new
> election, you would not see Chisholm, Bruce or Wells in
> the next House, and I have been told, from good authority,

---

[48] Upper Canada Courier, 4 June 1836.

that Waters and Chesser [sic] would also lose their seats.
The Highlanders of Glengarry are very indignant at the
majority of the present House.[49]

Although part of the indignation, especially among the Catholic Highlanders,

was the result of the Assembly's attack on Macdonell, the Orangemen

interpreted the feeling as a welcome expression of loyal enthusiasm.[50]

The Bishop gave particular consideration to the County of Stormont.

Archibald McLean was persuaded not to seek re-election in Cornwall, but

to stand for the County which he had formerly represented in several

Parliaments. At this point, Macdonell issued an "Address to the Catholic

and Protestant Free holders of the Counties of Stormont and Glengarry,"

which his friend Thomas Dalton published for him.[51] He briefly recounted

the history of the settlers of the Eastern District, emphasizing the

various favours, especially in land grants, which they had received from

the government, largely through his efforts and their proven loyalty.

And if you believe that I still have your interest at
heart, and that I know better than yourselves the most
effectual means of promoting it, you will elect men to
represent you in the ensuing Parliament of sound and
loyal principles, who have the real good of the country
at heart, who will not allow themselves to be duped or

---

[49] O.A., Ogle Gowan Papers, Gowan to James R. Gowan, 4 March 1836.

[50] Upper Canada Courier, 4 June, 18 June 1836. This aspect of the
campaign has been well covered by W.B. Kerr's excellent article, "When
Orange and Green United, 1832-39; The Alliance of Macdonell and Gowan",
Ontario Historical Society, Papers and Records, Vol. XXXIV, 1942. Gerald
Craig, op. cit., p. 238, suggests that one-third to one-half of the
Reform defeats were the result of this Orange-Catholic cooperation,
through their mutual support of candidates of each group.

[51] Toronto Patriot, 17 June 1836. It seems a gross oversimplification
to attribute this address, as does Sydney Jackman, Galloping Head, (London,
1958), p. 87, to the fact that ". . . the politics of the Bishop are easy
to understand, since Sir Francis had refused to accede to the Radical's
demand for his resignation from the Legislative Council".

misled by wicked hypocritical radicals, who are endeavouring
to drive the Province into rebellion, and to cut off every
connection between Canada and Great Britain, your Mother
Country, and to subject you to the domination of Yankee
rulers and Lynch Law.

Having thus described the alternatives open to the voters,

Macdonell continued his election sermon by praising Sir Francis Bond Head

as a true reformer, and flailing those members of the so-called Reform

Party who "assail him like hellhounds, with every possible abuse, indignity

and insult; and your late Representatives are joined in politics and

friendship with these Radical worthies". It was to line their own pockets

that the Reformers stopped the supplies, "and thereby prevented the issue

of the money which was to be laid out on public roads, canals and other

improvements in the Province".[52] It was an effective performance; and

most of the Tory newspapers credited Macdonell with ensuring the victory

of McLean over William Bruce, one of the leading Reformers of the

District.[53] Elsewhere the trend was the same. In Prescott, Chesser

and Waters, the Reformers, were replaced by John Kearns and Richard

P. Hotham. George Jarvis was successful in Cornwall, holding McLean's

former seat. Dundas and Russell Counties were both won by Constitution-

alists. The only disappointment for Macdonell in the Eastern District

was in his home County of Glengarry. Donald Aeneas Macdonell was re-

turned again, but so also was Alexander Chisholm, the Bishop's "radical

---

[52]Ibid.

[53]Kerr, op. cit., p. 39.

cousin". It is debatable whether this was not simply a personal or clan antipathy. Chisholm held his militia colonelcy through the rebellion.[54] Macdonell could be well pleased with the result of his most dramatic foray into an election.

In appreciation of the Bishop's role in defense of the government, the Orangemen cancelled their annual parade on July 12, and instead drank toasts to his patriotism. Editor O'Grady almost had apoplexy at this unholy alliance, and he railed against the intervention of these "state-paid priests".[55] But Macdonell, of course, would never concede that taking the field against Mackenzie was an intervention in politics. For him there was no proper distinction to be made between political man and the total man. Allegiance to God, King and Country were indivisible characteristics of the good subject. He had been perfectly candid about this when he had replied that very spring to the charges of Mackenzie in the Assembly. As their Bishop it was his imperative duty to instill

> . . . in the minds of my flock principles of attachment
> and loyalty to their Sovereign and the Constitution of
> their Country and thus prevent [Mackenzie's] mischievous
> endeavours to alienate their minds from the one and the
> other by his Revolutionary and Rebellious harangues and
> writings. If this be a crime, it is a crime for which
> I never can expect forgiveness. So far indeed from
> repenting of it that neither Racks nor Gibbets shall
> ever deter me from persevering in such a Sacred duty.[56]

---

[54] Campbell, "Members of the House of Assembly for Upper Canada", Transactions of the Royal Society, 1910, p. 188; for Chisholm, see, W.L. Scott, "Glengarry's Representatives in the Legislative Assembly of Upper Canada", Canadian Catholic Historical Association, Annual Report, 1939-40, p. 42.

[55] Correspondent and Advocate, 27 July, 3 August 1836; and St. Thomas Liberal, cited in Craig, op. cit., p. 239.

[56] A.A.K., Macdonell Papers, Macdonell to Joseph, 7 March 1836.

This unshakeable conviction in the righteousness of his course sustained him throughout his life; but at the same time made him almost impervious to any suggestion that there might be some merit in the views of those who disagreed with him. If Mackenzie's ideas were wicked and disloyal, then those of all Reformers were unacceptable. Thus, in a subsequent pastoral letter, he commended his people, that "at the last general election, you rallied round the Government, and contributed in a great degree, to turn out the avowed enemies of the British Constitution".[57] Not only had they acted wisely in doing so, but in accordance with their duty, since "your loyalty is based on the Sacred obligations of your Holy Religion. The apostle commands us to obey and be submissive to the powers that be".[58]

For Macdonell, then, the election of 1836 had restored the province to its accustomed state of loyalty and tranquillity, thus undoing the machinations of Mackenzie and redeeming the people from their aberrant behaviour of 1834. With the Constitutionalists now firmly in control of all branches of the legislature, Upper Canada could resume its orderly progress in true liberty and prosperity. As for himself, he had once again demonstrated his ability to rally his flock in defense of constituted authority.

---

[57] Ibid., "The Address of Bishop Macdonell to the Irish Catholics of Upper Canada".

[58] Ibid.

CHAPTER VI

ON THE BARRICADES

I

For over a year after the election of 1836, Bishop Macdonell's
life took on an even tenor. His co-adjutor had relieved him of most
of the administrative load of the Diocese of Kingston. Retirement
seemed most attractive; but there was still the nagging problem of
the seminary and how to ensure that it was adequately financed on a permanent basis. If he could accomplish this last task, he would be content.
The Catholic Church was flourishing; its congregations augmented annually
by the continuing flow of emigrants from Ireland. Such an institution
would be a fitting capstone to a career in which he had almost single-
handedly established his religion in Upper Canada. Macdonell knew well
enough that resources were limited. It would be years before the
Catholic population, almost all of them new farmers and town labourers,
would be able to contribute significantly to its maintenance. They
could do little enough in supporting their local pastors and churches.

The only solution was an endowment. It would have to come either
from government or as a result of a personal fund-raising journey back
home, or more likely, a combination of both. While he may have longed
to visit Scotland once more, he was now seventy-four years of age, and
the rigours of such a journey at his age gave him pause. The former

possibility, a government endowment, would mean continued effort in the cultivation of the authorities at Toronto, and especially the new Lieutenant Governor. The Bishop's timely appeal to his flock during the election had brought him to Head's attention, and Macdonell was now well versed in using his reputation for loyalty to advantage.

But whether willingly or not, he would soon find himself drawn into the turmoil of the rebellion and its aftermath. His departure for the British Isles would have to be postponed. It is unlikely, however, that Macdonell regretted the role he was to play in 1837 and throughout the following year. He had never forgotten his martial career at the close of the old century. It was a vanity of his, and perhaps forgiveable, that even at his time of life he could once again call his Highlanders to the defense of their country. If the outcome of the election had to be confirmed by force of arms, it would put a final end to those wicked attempts to overturn the Constitution. It never occurred to Bishop Macdonell (or to most Upper Canadian Tories) that it was not only the radicals who lost in 1837. The threat posed at Montgomery's Tavern by Mackenzie and his pathetic band of followers was symptomatic of a deeper malaise, and a portent. Macdonell died before the full implications of that skirmish became known. It was enough for him that he was able, once more, to rally his people to the cause of the Queen and constituted authority.

II

The Tories of the Province, including Macdonell, had received the election results of the summer of 1836 with satisfaction. Their

stand had been vindicated at the polls, and they could return to their

 normal pursuits. The Bishop turned his attention to consolidating his

position with the Lieutenant Governor. His influence would be necessary

if the scheme for the seminary was to be moved forward. It is not at

all surprising that neither his strategy nor his tactics changed. The

political crisis so happily weathered demonstrated that conservative

success depended upon a mutually sustaining coalition focussed on the

Lieutenant Governor. If previously, Macdonell had been considered use-

ful to the Compact, then surely his recent effectiveness made him even

more necessary to the administration.

He had no hesitation, therefore, in recommending Catholics, such

as John MacConnell, for positions as magistrates, on grounds that he

"exerted with great effort at the last Election in favour of the Con-

stitutional candidate".[1] When Head sent him an advance copy of his

address to the newly-elected Assembly, Macdonell's reply was a thinly-

veiled indication that he believed his own stock had risen.[2] If

Macdonell required any further confirmation, he was reassured by Head's

generosity a few months later   In his reply to the Lieutenant Governor,

Macdonell wrote

> I cannot find words strong enough to express the grateful
> sense I entertain of the goodness and kind condescension
> of His Excellency towards me since his arrival in this
> Province, and the last proof he gave of his liberality

---

[1] P.A.C., Upper Canada Sundries, Macdonell to Joseph, 5 November 1836.

[2] Ibid., Macdonell to Head, 15 November 1836.

and goodness towards the Catholics of Toronto in granting
a Block of land in the western part of the city for a
church and Presbytery for them, and the honor he has conferred on me by calling it Macdonell Square has made an
impression on my mind which time can never efface.[3]

Now that he was on good terms with Head, Macdonell had his friend
Anthony Manahan, one of the new members for Hastings, introduce a bill
into the Assembly for the incorporation of the seminary, to be called
Regiopolis College. It moved through the House and the Legislative
Council without difficulty.[4] John Strachan voted for the bill, but did
not speak to it. Indeed, there was very little discussion at all.[5]

The Bishop had not expected much opposition on this score. It
would be much less easy to persuade the government to grant funds to
the institution; but the ground-work had to be laid. He was now resigned
to the necessity of a trip to the British Isles to solicit money, and
by early 1837, had determined to leave as soon as possible. The Bishop
of Montreal, Jean-Jacques Lartigue, invited Macdonell to visit him
before he took ship. Lartigue also requested permission to distribute
the Bishop's election address in French.[6] Since he was a cousin of
Papineau and D.-B. Viger, Lartigue was considerably worried about his
reputation with the British authorities. It was necessary, he said, to

---

[3]P.A.C., R.G.5, C2, Provincial Secretary's Office, Vol. 5, No. 539, Macdonell to Joseph, 27 April 1837.

[4]Upper Canada, House of Assembly, Journal, 1836-37, p. 530; Journal of the Legislative Council, 1837, pp. 207,217.

[5]P.A.C., CO42, Head to Glenelg, 17 July 1837.

[6]R.A.Q., 1945-46, Correspondence of Lartigue, Lartigue to Macdonell 15 January 1837, p. 90.

be "trés forts contre rebellion envers le pouvoir civil, afin de faire voir l'unanimité des évêques sur ce point".[7]

Shortly after this, Macdonell received a letter from Lieutenant Governor, Sir John Harvey, of New Brunswick indicating the latter's objections to the appointment of a French Canadian to the vacant bishopric of his province. Harvey requested Macdonell's intervention in Rome and London.[8] Macdonell complied, and with considerable effect, for the new Bishop of New Brunswick was Donald MacDonald, of Prince Edward Island. Ecclesiastical affairs generally, preoccupied Bishop Macdonell throughout the spring and summer of 1837. There was a strong movement underway to have North America declared an Ecclesiastical Province in its own right, to which the American Bishops agreed. Since this involved not only negotiations with Rome, but the delicate problem of civil (i.e. British) recognition of the Bishop of Quebec as metropolitan, Macdonell was desired by the Lower Canadian hierarchy to lead the negotiations. Accordingly, Macdonell made an extended journey to Montreal and Quebec City, where he had long discussions with Lord Gosford, the Governor General. He succeeded in persuading Gosford to open the subject with London, and give his approbation. Lartigue seemed well pleased with this beginning and informed Signay, Bishop of Quebec, that "le gouverneur a donné de bonnes espérances à Mgr. de Kingston pour l'établissement d'une province

---

[7] Ibid.

[8] Vatican Archives, *Archivio della Propaganda Fide*, 1837, Acta IV, Harvey to Macdonell, 30 April 1837; Macdonell to Weld, 16 June 1837. [Originals in English].

ecclésiastique, mais non sans quelque délai".[9] Macdonell must have
wished that his influence was as great with the government at Toronto.

He was assured, however, of his standing in Glengarry. Before
he had gone to Montreal, the Catholics of the Eastern District had
invited him to St. Andrews to celebrate the fiftieth anniversary of his
ordination as a priest; and Macdonell chose to celebrate his jubilee
among his countrymen rather than at Montreal to which he had also been
invited for the occasion. The newspaper account noted that over 2,000
people gathered to hear the Bishop's address, in which he described himself as "the humble instrument of procuring for them the many temporal
and spiritual advantages which they at present enjoy".[10] It was a warm
and sentimental event for the Bishop, and confirmed his resolve that he
should leave his church well provided for when his ministry was ended.

But when he arrived back in Kingston in the early autumn of 1837,
he did not find the calm complacency which had settled over the province
briefly after the last election. The depression which afflicted both
sides of the Atlantic was causing severe hardship. Sir Francis Bond Head
was rapidly losing the confidence of the conservatives through his
curious attitudes toward economic affairs, especially banking. The
failure of Lord Gosford's mission to Lower Canada had prompted a new
sternness from the Colonial Office toward the lower province. And

---

[9] R.A.Q., Correspondence of Lartigue, Lartigue to Signay, 17 August
1837, p. 248.

[10] Kingston Chronicle, 25 February 1837.

William Lyon Mackenzie, in furious indignation, was attacking randomly,
the Lieutenant Governor, banks, the Colonial Office and even Bishop
Macdonell in his campaign to lead the people of Upper Canada into his
vision of an agrarian utopia. With the moderate reformers such as
Bidwell and Robert Baldwin now withdrawn from political life, Mackenzie's
extremism provoked a like response. As an example of the kind of conditioned rhetoric this distracted situation produced a Kingstonian came
to Macdonell's defense in a letter to Head. "He is loyal to the back-
bone; and, in the late war, led the Glengarry Militia in the field,
bearing, as the Americans said, a charmed life. He is well-known to
some of the members of the Royal Family; and altogether, although exceedingly disliked by the American Party, is beloved and esteemed by every
respectable person of every other party and of every creed in Canada."[11]
Macdonell's own concerns were now to be lost, for a while, in the
excitement of Mackenzie's ill-fated adventure.

There was, of course, no question as to what position he would
take. But it is a much more difficult task to determine what he thought
had caused the resort to extremities. There are only two documents which
provide much insight into his private feelings about the course of events
in Upper Canada. The first is a letter he wrote in March, 1838, to
Lieutenant General, Sir John Macdonald, the Adjutant General in London,
with whom he had campaigned in Ireland at the turn of the century. It

---

[11]R.H.B. to Head, 5 November 1837; cited in Sir Richard H. Bonnycastle,
Canada, as it was, is, and may be, 2 vols. (London, 1852), I, pp. 269-70.
R.H.B. was likely either Richard Bullock, High Sheriff of Kingston, or
perhaps Bonnycastle himself.

is generally thought that Mackenzie's support was weak and isolated; that the flag of rebellion brought out thousands--on the side of the government. Macdonell suggested, however, "That the present state of the Canadas is anything but secure. The poison which Mackenzie and Papineau and their rebel associates have so extensively infused into the minds of the people of both Provinces has taken too deep a root to expect that it will be eradicated in a short time".[12]

If Mackenzie had succeeded in burning Toronto, "which mere accident prevented him from doing", Macdonell continued, a great majority of the people would have joined him. This was especially true of the people surrounding Kingston, "who consist principally of Americans". Only the continued presence of troops would keep down disaffection.

> Our present Lieutenant Governor, Sir Francis Bondhead [sic] returns home loaded with addresses of thanks from all classes of the population of the Province. Yet his administration has not been without censure, indeed I do not believe but it is impossible for any man to administer the Govert. of Upper Canada in a manner to give satisfaction to all parties, so jarring are the various interests in the Province. But of all the causes of envy, jealousies and discontents, the greatest and most fertile source is the question of the Clergy Reserves, and until that be decided I do not hesitate to predict that there will never be perfect tranquillity in Upper Canada.[13]

---

[12]P.A.C., Macdonell Papers, Macdonell to Lt. General Sir John Macdonald, 10 March 1838, pp. 25, 30. This small collection of letters, all dated between 1834-39, are typescript copies of letters that were in the Archdiocesan Archives at Kingston. The originals are no longer there among the Bishop's papers. This particular letter is addressed to Sir John Macdonald, but it is a transcription error. The Bishop had two friends, both Generals at the time, Sir John Macdonald, and Major General Sir James Macdonell, who came to North America in 1838 as Brigade Commander of the troops which accompanied the new Governor General. He later became Commander of the Forces in British North America, until 1841 when he was promoted Lieutenant General. Internal evidence in this letter makes it quite clear that the addressee was Sir John Macdonald, the Adjutant General in London.

[13]Ibid., as are all intervening citations.

The reflection on Sir Francis is interesting, corroborating Professor
Craig's suggestion that the Tories were not at all pleased with Head's
stubborn performance after the rebellion.[14] The reference to the Clergy
Reserves is more traditional. It was obviously a crucial and provocative
issue; but, Macdonell, of course, had a strong vested interest in its
outcome.

The second document, a letter to Lord Durham three months later,
was intended partly for effect, but written "fearlessly and unhesitatingly,
with such information as my opportunities have enabled me to acquire".[15]
Macdonell claimed that because of the exhortations of himself and his
clergy scarcely a Catholic, Irish or Scot, was involved in the rebellion.

> The leaders and chief contrivers of the late outbreak were
> Protestants, Presbyterians and Methodists; but the majority
> of the rebels were Methodists and Presbyterians. Such of
> the Protestants as became disaffected and inimical to the
> Govert., are so from jealousy and disappointment at seeing
> a certain party in and about Toronto assume too much power
> and exercise what they think too much influence over the
> different Lieut. Governors [sic] so much so that there is
> hardly a situation of trust or emolument but what is engaged
> by themselves and their friends.
>
> The Methodists and Presbyterians are become disaffected
> from their Dread and abhorrence of a dominant Church. . . .[16]

Combining the two letters, what can be said about Macdonell's
interpretation? First of all, Mackenzie's rebellious challenge to duly

---

[14]Craig, op. cit., pp. 242-43.

[15]P.A.C., Macdonell Papers, Macdonell to Durham, 14 June 1838,
p. 32. See also Sir C.P. Lucas, (ed.), Lord Durham's Report on the
Affairs of British North America, 3 volumes, (Oxford, 1912), Vol. III,
Appendixes, pp. 18-21.

[16]Ibid.

constituted authority must be resisted. As a Tory (or, for that matter, as a Whig), he must decry such violent madness. The reference to American influence was a stock response of most conservatives in Upper Canada to dissent. Some of Sir Francis Bond Head's more intransigent reactions were to be deplored. But Macdonell also suggests that discontent was widespread in the Province, and probably not without cause. As we shall note later, even Catholics were similarly unhappy at some aspects of the current administration.[17] There remains, however, one other theme to this discontent which becomes sharply focussed. The claim that Church of England Tories monopolized place and influence, the exacerbating question of the Clergy Reserves and the pretensions of the Church of England to be the established church in the province read like the catalogue of criticism which Marshall Spring Bidwell and other moderate Reformers had been directing at the executive for years.

Such an analogy would have horrified Macdonell. But considered from this point of view, it tends to throw into relief the problems of one who does not share the assumptions or accept the convictions of the inner core of Upper Canadian Toryism for whatever reason. Common ground on these issues (though not, of course, their resolution) could be found by people as disparate as Bishop Macdonell, Peter Perry, the Reformer, William Morris, the conservative spokesman of the Church of Scotland,

---

[17] For example, one could note here in Lucas, op. cit., that the Table of Contents of Appendix A of Durham's Report lists an unprinted "Memorial of Anthony Manahan, Esq. complaining of the total exclusion of all Roman Catholics (Irish) from all places of emolument and honour in the power of the Government of Upper Canada". Manahan was Macdonell's spokesman in the Assembly.

Egerton Ryerson, or, to take it to the absurd, William Lyon Mackenzie.
In the exciting years of the 1830's, Bishop Macdonell was a Tory and a
defiant opponent of radicalism; but perceiving, from his own peculiar
vantage point, some of the same weaknesses and failings as did the
Reformers in a system of government he fought mightily to defend. If
his position was anomalous, somehow out of joint with reality, so perhaps
was the system.

III

During the first few months of 1838, despite his seventy-six years,
Macdonell took an avid interest in the military preparations going forward.
The destruction of the Caroline, on the American bank of the Niagara
River, had thrown the whole frontier area of New York State into great
excitement, and fears of invasion were rife. Allan MacNab was knighted
for cutting out the Caroline, but the Bishop did not think much of the
escapade, nor of the capacity of the American government to control its
citizens.

> I doubt the will and I deny the power of the authorities
> in that State to get back the arms and ammunitions from
> Navy Island; and the rash act of destroying the Steamboat
> Caroline has infuriated the minds of the people along the
> whole line of the frontier to such a degree that they only
> want leaders to burst into Canada in different parts.
> Our safety hitherto has been in a great degree owing to
> the intervention of kind Providence, and the continued
> openess of this extraordinary winter shows that our pro-
> tection is in more powerful hands than those of our
> temporal rulers.[18]

---

[18]P.A.C., Macdonell Papers, Macdonell to Manahan, 8 January 1838,
p. 18.

To his old friend Sir John Colborne, now Commander of the Forces,
he confided his lack of confidence in the military capacity of Upper
Canada's leadership. The province, in fact, had only been saved by a
stroke of fortune, or, as Macdonell put it

> To the kind intervention of Divine Providence alone we
> are indebted for the preservation of Toronto. Had
> Mackenzie's fighting General Anderson not been thrown
> off his horse and broken his neck at the moment he was
> putting his rebel bands in motion to march into the city,
> there is not the least doubt that Toronto would have
> been taken and plundered, but the providential death of
> that rebel disconcerted Mackenzie, deranged his plans,
> discouraged his followers and saved Toronto. Had
> Mackenzie, Rolph and Duncombe been secured, as they might
> easily have been, peace and tranquility [sic] might be
> in as fair a way of being restored to the loyal inhabitants
> of this Province as to those of Lower Canada, but in
> place of that, I am greatly afraid that our troubles
> and our dangers are only commencing.[19]

But the root problem, he continued, is that the majority of the
population are undependable, loyal only so long as the government appears
to be in control of the situation; "should the rebels get a footing in
the Province many thousands of them would join the enemy". Only an
efficient internal defence would guarantee the security of Upper Canada.
The best and cheapest manner of accomplishing that end would be to raise
a number of fencible corps and pay them with unconceded crown lands.
He had suggested this as long ago as 1802, to Lord Sidmouth, he reminded
Colborne. Had it been adopted it would have saved the expenditure of
many millions, and provided quite adequate defence. He concluded his
letter somewhat gloomily, by observing that "We feel in perfect security

---

[19] P.A.C., Colborne Papers, Vol. 12, Macdonell to Colborne,
8 January 1838, pp. 3555-57.

in Kingston with Colonel Cubitt commanding the garrison, and Colonel
Bonnycastle the Militia of the District. But for those two active and
experienced officers we could show but a feeble defence to an invading
enemy under our superanuated [sic] Colonels of Militia, and hesitating
and undecisive magistrates".[20]

Perhaps it was his age that made him querulous, but Macdonell
flung out some startling charges. He virtually accused John Solomon
Cartwright and John Macaulay of "having obtained from the Lieutenant
Governor the freedom of the Arch Rebel [Mackenzie?], because, as it is
rumoured, he was indebted to the Commercial Bank, that he would not be
able to pay if he was tried and found guilty of treason".[21] Kingston
was greatly endangered, because "Sir Francis robbed the town of the
arms that were deposited in it for its defence. Our rulers have much
to answer for, for neglect, omission and mismanagement".[22] But the alarums
passed and Kingston and Upper Canada survived. As the invasion threat
receded, so also did Macdonell's frustration at what he felt was military
ineptitude all about him. There was now time to resume planning for his
seminary and the journey to Europe, and to keep an eye cocked to the
doings of the politicians in Toronto.

He had many friends (and relatives) in the House, now, and the
ease by which he had secured the charter of incorporation for the seminary

---

[20]Ibid., as are the intervening citations.

[21]P.A.C., Macdonell Papers, Macdonell to Manahan, 20 February
1838, p. 19.

[22]Ibid.

augured well. Early in 1838, his old associate from Stormont, Archibald McLean, with Manahan, introduced a motion to expunge the censure that had been passed on himself and Strachan by the former Assembly.[23] Anthony Manahan was busy at other matters as well. It was he who gave notice of a motion to appeal to the Queen for the union of Upper and Lower Canada,[24] almost immediately after the rebellions. There is no evidence that Macdonell declared himself one way or the other on this question. But there was a strong suspicion, on the part of the Quebec Bishops at least, that he favoured such a project. It was well known that he and Manahan were close friends. They both lived in Kingston which had flirted with the idea of union in 1822 because of the interest of the commercial men of the town in the development of the St. Lawrence. And now he was planning to visit the British Isles, and very probably the Colonial Office. The Bishop of Quebec, in fact, was under the impression that "en compagnie d'autres citoyens de Kingston, [Macdonell] avait lui-même pétitionné en faveur de l'union".[25]

In fact, Macdonell again postponed his voyage to Europe. A year later, when he once more announced his departure, the Quebec hierarchy were still apprehensive. They had always maintained a healthy

---

[23] Upper Canada, House of Assembly, Journal, 1837-38, 6 January 1838, p. 54; see also P.A.C., Macdonell Papers, Macdonell to Manahan, 8 January 1838, p. 19, in which he sends his thanks.

[24] Upper Canada, House of Assembly, Journal, 1837-38, 30 December 1837, p. 23.

[25] Signay to Lartigue, 11 February 1838, cited in Lemieux, op. cit., pp. 440-41.

respect for the Bishop's influence at the Colonial Office, and, indeed often sought his support for their projects. They were greatly opposed to the proposed union. Bishop Turgeon wrote to Bourget, in his anxiety about Macdonell's trip, that "Je pense que ce serait un moyen bien expéditif de nous faire Américains. Nos radicaux réunis à ceux du Haut-Canada auraient bientôt terminé cette affaire".[26] It is unfortunate that Macdonell is not on record on this issue. He left Upper Canada before it became a divisive political struggle, even among conservatives. Very likely, however, given his situation, he would not have been antipathetic.

As the spring of 1838 approached, Macdonell's mind was on other concerns. A new Lieutenant Governor was coming. Sir Francis had written personally to the Bishop to inform him that he was "about to quit this terrible life", and to thank him for being "my constant and fearless supporter".[27] Once again the Colonial wheel was turning. As an example of the type of rumour-mongering that always preceded such a change, Macdonell noted in his letter to Lt. General Sir John Macdonald, "The unfavourable reports that are spreading through the Province of the despotic character of our new Lt. Governor, Sir George Arthur, seem to occasion alarm to many of the well disposed inhabitants, although others are willing to believe that the circulation of those reports may be

---

[26] Ibid., Turgeon to Bourget, 29 January 1839.

[27] Corbett, op. cit., pp. 54-55, Head to Macdonell, 16 February 1838.

attributed to the malice of Mackenzie and his Yankie [sic] friends".[28]
Considering the warm and fruitful relationship which the Bishop had with
Arthur the foreboding appears comic. But even more important, a new
Governor General was arriving as well, invested with sweeping powers as
High Commissioner to investigate and recommend changes in the system of
government which had apparently proved so unsatisfactory as to provoke
rebellion. Both events would have to be attended with care.

Macdonell was on hand to help welcome Sir George Arthur on his
first visit to Kingston; and his name headed a long list of clergymen,
magistrates and local dignitaries on the address of welcome.[29] The
Bishop was contemplating a journey to the Lower Province to meet Durham
as well. Archdeacon John Strachan was also concerned about the import
of Durham's broad powers. He was launching another, and finally successful, petition to be elevated to a Bishopric in Upper Canada.[30] When
Strachan heard that Macdonell planned to visit Durham in Montreal, he
wrote to the Bishop, admitting he had little influence with the new
Governor General. But he hoped that Macdonell would represent his interests to Durham; and give him

. . . if encouraged a copy of the letter which you had
the goodness to write on my behalf to Lord Glenelg. In

---

[28]P.A.C., Macdonell Papers, Macdonell to Macdonald, 10 March 1838.

[29]P.A.C., Upper Canada Sundries, address printed 24 May 1838.

[30]Ibid. Petition of Archdeacon John Strachan, 14 May 1838. In
his catalogue of testimonials Strachan noted 'I have always been on the
most friendly and intimate terms with Bishop McDonell, the head of the
Roman Catholic Church'.

regard to my sentiments and policy on most subjects you
know them as I do myself for they are in the main fully
accordant with your own. Sincere attachment to the
Parent State--Justice, kindness and perfect freedom of
conscience.[31]

Despite this warm, friendly letter, it does not appear that Macdonell

acted on the request, perhaps because of the Clergy Reserves.

In fact, he changed his tactics somewhat. He did not cancel

his visit to Montreal, but decided to write a long memorandum to Durham,

previously cited, before seeking an interview. After recounting what he

felt had precipitated the rebellion, Macdonell went on to suggest the

remedy necessary to tranquillize the province. The great, distracting

issue was that of the Clergy Reserves, and, of course, the right of

the Catholics to share in them.

The warm and animated discussion which has taken place
between the Archdeacon of Toronto and the Honourable
William Morris of Perth in reference to the right of
the Presbyterians to a share of the Clergy Reserves
has raised a general excitement among the Presbyterians
which will take a long time to allay and may terminate
in unpleasant if not in dangerous results.[32]

The Catholics, Macdonell continued, "who compose a great pro-

portion of the population of Upper Canada", were also dissatisfied; the

Irish Catholics, especially, who arrived with memories of tythes and

rack rents, and a "mortal hatred to Orangeism which they find so rapidly

---

[31]P.A.C., Strachan Papers, Letter Book 3, Strachan to Macdonell,
7 June 1838. The great exceptions, of course, were Clergy Reserves and
Establishment. But there is no evidence that the two ever discussed
these issues between themselves. They were the unspoken, but ever-
present, barrier to full accord.

[32]P.A.C., Macdonell Papers, Macdonell to Durham, 14 June 1838,
pp. 31-34.

spreading over this Province". They are thus susceptible to any demagogue who preys on their fears. Since they are poor, they cannot build churches and schools, and become "disappointed and annoyed at being excluded from their share of the Clergy Reserves". There were abundant funds in the province from the disposal of the school lands and the Reserves; and it is "the witholding of those funds and the spread of the Orange system" which "are the principal, if not the only grounds of discontent among all denominations in Upper Canada". The Catholic clergy, in addition, had a special claim, Macdonell concluded. Since the original purpose of the confiscated Jesuit Estates in Lower Canada was for instruction of the Indians in the Christian religion, a share of that property should go toward aiding the Catholic church in Upper Canada in this missionary endeavour. This was particularly important, because the "Methodists have so disgusted the Indians by interference with their temporal concerns, contrary to the practice of the Catholic Clergy who confine themselves entirely to spiritual matters".[33]

It was, of course, quite natural for Macdonell to seize upon the Reserves question as a major source of irritation. But the letter is worthy of note for its omissions as well. There is no hint of criticism of the structure of the government of Upper Canada. No reference is made to the issue of "responsibility", currently being debated; and more important, no reflection on the manner in which public affairs are conducted. In other words, despite Macdonell's awareness of the sources

---

[33]Ibid., as all intervening citations.

of discontent, he seems to feel that if the monopoly of the Church of England over the Reserves is broken, all will be well. It must be added, that the Bishop was seeking the best advantage of his church and his people. However, it is curious that he did not remark upon the exclusiveness of the patronage system, as he had when discussing the background of the rebellion; although he would hardly go so far as Charles Buller, Durham's associate, who described the Family Compact as a "petty, corrupt insolent Tory clique",[34] to use his oft-quoted epithet.

Perhaps, from his own point of view, however, Macdonell's concentration on the vexatious Clergy Reserves was justified. It was certainly reflected in Durham's scorching indictment in his Report, and the particular attention he gave to Macdonell's representations about the situation of Catholics generally.[35] This is not to suggest that the Bishop's influence with Durham was extraordinary; but Macdonell's letter was one of the very few, among a multitude, which the High Commissioner chose to include in his Report. Macdonell went down to the Lower Province late in June, but there is no record of a meeting with Durham.[36]

In any case, after he returned home to Kingston, the Bishop abandoned his campaign for a direct share in the Clergy Reserves. Taking up the alternative he had considered previously, he requested the

---

[34]Quoted in Chester New, Lord Durham, (London, 1929), pp. 403-04.

[35]Lucas, op. cit., Vol. II, pp. 177, 179-82.

[36]P.A.C., MG 24, A 27, Durham Papers, Vol. 26, Quiblier (Superior of the Seminary of Quebec) to Durham, 21 June 1838, requesting an interview. There is no indication of Durham's response.

Lieutenant Governor, Sir George Arthur,

> . . . to mention to his Lordship the Earl of Durham that
> it is my intention to induce the Catholics of Upper
> Canada to relinquish their claim to a share of the Clergy
> Reserves of this Province provided they get a grant of
> the property formerly belonging to the Jesuits in Lower
> Canada. As this property had been granted originally for
> promoting catholic education and instructing the Indians
> in the principles of Christianity I hope Her Majesty
> will be graciously pleased to grant it to us.[37]

Arthur was more than pleased at Macdonell's decision as it removed at
least one obstacle "to a satisfactory adjustment of the long agitated
question of the Clergy Reserves".[38] And, as the Bishop had probably
guessed, predisposed the Lieutenant Governor toward other Catholic claims.
Arthur made clear his sense of obligation that the government must
cultivate religion and piety.[39]

But once more, Macdonell, and Upper Canada were distracted by
violence. Rebellion broke out again in Lower Canada in the wake of
Durham's departure; and border incursions by the "Patriots" threw the
upper province into a state of alarm. In response to Arthur's request
that he delay his trip to England, Macdonell replied, that "As your
Excellency has been pleased to say that my stay might be of some use to
the Province during the impending invasion I have put off my departure
for the present".[40] It was necessary, he advised Arthur "unhesitatingly",

---

[37] P.A.C., Upper Canada Sundries, Macdonell to Arthur, 4 October 1838.

[38] C.K. Sanderson (ed.), The Arthur Papers, 3 vols. (Toronto, 1957),
Arthur to Macdonell, 19 October 1838, I, pp. 307-08.

[39] Ibid.

[40] P.A.C., Macdonell Papers, Macdonell to Arthur, 29 October 1838,
p. 37.

to appoint corps commanders who had the confidence of the people, and
the Bishop was happy to recommend Mr. McDonell of Peterboro for such
a situation. His own services were offered as well

> Should your Excellency determine to raise a corps of
> Irish Catholics under the command of Col. Baldwin of
> the Gore of Toronto, I would pledge my life that your
> Excellency cannot muster a more loyal, more gallant,
> or a more efficient corps in this or any other Province,
> and old and stiff as I am, I am willing and ready to go
> to Toronto to attend them.[41]

From any man of seventy-six years of age but Macdonell, the offer would
be ludicrous.

Sir George Arthur declined comment on the Bishop's martial zeal,
but he was prepared to take his advice on appointments.

> Your recommendation of your friend, Colonel McDonnel
> [i.e. Macdonell of Peterborough], I attended to as soon
> as I received it, and if only he can meet with a body
> of brigands the field of Glory will be open to him!
>
> Your friend Captain Wilson, (London District) has
> applied for the office of Clerk of the Peace to which
> I have this day appointed him. His application was
> accompanied by a Letter which Your Lordship had
> addressed to him eighteen months ago--but you will
> see it had not lost its "value".[42]

To Macdonell it was only fair that military and other appointments should
reflect the pluralism of the province, and he kept a sharp eye on announcements. When he suspected that John Solomon Cartwright, M.P.P., and
president of the Commerical Bank in Kingston, was impeding the advancement of Captain Archibald Macdonald, the Bishop wrote tartly to "my dear

---

[41] Ibid.

[42] Sanderson, _Arthur Papers_, Arthur to Macdonell, 6 December 1838,
I, pp. 419-420. Parentheses included.

Cartwright, to tell you what I dare say you are aware of yourself that a system of favouritism and partiality has brought all the evils upon this Province, under which it now groans, and that it is time it should come to an end".[43]

But it was not as a military advisor that Bishop Macdonell could best respond usefully to the renewed crisis. He knew what was expected of him. He composed an address to the inhabitants of the County of Glengarry, which was printed and distributed throughout the Eastern District. The Highland tradition of military service to the Empire was well known, he began, and there "is no doubt in my mind that you will turn out to a man on the present occasion and join with your loyal fellow subjects in defence of your wives and children against the attacks of a heartless gang of pirates and rebels".[44] He assured his countrymen that their loyalty would not be presumed upon lightly in an exhortation that was equally directed at the authorities in Toronto.

> It is not a little to your credit, Glengarry men, Catholics and Protestants, that you have carefully abstained from entering into the existing overheated and certainly, in the present critical state of the Province, unreasonable discussion of your claims upon Govert. Fear not, my friends, that you whose fathers has [sic] been so much distinguished in the conquest of the Canadas, and who have yourselves contributed so powerfully to the defense of them from foreign and domestic enemies, shall be forgotten by a grateful and generous Sovereign in the distribution of rewards.

---

[43] P.A.C., Macdonell Papers, Macdonell to Cartwright, 21 November 1838.

[44] P.A.C., Macdonell Papers, "The Address of Bishop Macdonell to the Inhabitants of the County of Glengarry", Kingston, 1 November 1838, pp. 38-40.

Macdonell closed with a prayer "That the God of Battles may be your

Protector, and grant success to the righteousness of your cause".[45]

As he had indicated on former occasions, the Bishop could be relied

upon to rouse his people, but there was a clear indication that their

claims could not be denied.

Sir George Arthur conveyed his thanks for "a copy of your admir-

able address, and I am much gratified to find that it is your intention

to publish one of the same kind to the Irish Roman Catholics".[46] In

fact, the Bishop had already done so a week earlier. The Irish Catholics

were now, by far, the largest proportion of his flock, and he wished to

use the opportunity to sum up their experience in the province and indi-

cate their prospects. Conscious of the fact that as a Highlander he

could never be one with the Irish, he relied on their willingness to

heed the advice (if reasonable) of their spiritual leaders. This long

address is the best example of how Macdonell tried to cope with the pro-

blem of directing the often unruly Irish into loyal tractability. It

also illustrates the Bishop's rhetorical technique and selective use

of history.

The address begins with Macdonell's congratulations to the Irish

Catholics that the "Radicals and enemies of your Holy Religion" were

---

[45]Ibid., and intervening citations.

[46]Sanderson, Arthur Papers, Arthur to Macdonell, 6 December 1838,
p. 420.

frustrated in their attempts to make them rebels.[47] "How more prudent

your conduct has been than that of your countrymen, who in the years

of 1797-98, allowed themselves to be deluded by cunning and designing

men, who vainly thought to overturn the British Government in Ireland.

. . ." In Upper Canada, however, Irish loyalty and good conduct have

earned the confidence of the government, despite the prejudice which

existed against Irish immigration. It was the Bishop, himself, who

assured Lord Bathurst and the Colonial Office, in writing, that they

would be industrious and orderly.

> Yes, my friends I pledged my life for your good conduct--
> during the period of fifteen years, which have elapsed,
> since that pledge was given, I have had no cause to
> regret the confidence I placed in your honor and your
> loyalty.

While the attachment of other colonists to the British Consti-

tution might depend on the favours of government, the Bishop was sure

that "your loyalty is uncompromising, and based on the principles of

honor, and the sacred obligations inculcated by your Holy Religion".

The suspicion of the Catholic Irish as rebellious is misplaced, Macdonell

argued, since the Irish rebellion of 1798 was led by Protestants.

Napper Tandy, Hamilton Rowan, Wolfe Tone and Robert Emmet were all

Protestants who prodded into insurrection a people groaning under the

"galling yoke" of tythes and taxes and other obnoxious burdens. In

contrast, Macdonell pointed out approvingly the non-violent campaign of

---

[47]This, and succeeding quotations are from A.A.K., Macdonell
Papers, "The Address of Bishop Macdonell to the Irish Catholics of
Upper Canada", 1 December 1838. It was printed at the British Whig,
Kingston, and circulated throughout Upper Canada.

Daniel O'Connell. He did not, of course, mention the inconsistency of
it all; that the plight of the Irish at home existed under the British
Constitution, and that the "galling yoke" went on no matter what tactics
were adopted.

Macdonell then turned to the French Canadians. Those contented
people were deluded by "Irreligious Papineau, Atheistical Giraud and
Camelion [sic] O'Callaghan" who harped on imagined grievances. That
"unfledged gang of briefless lawyers, notaries and other pettifoggers"
seduced the poor, credulous Canadians to line their own pockets. The
Bishop went on to describe, at length, the stormy and bloody history of
attempts to establish republican governments. It was especially notorious
in South America, with "Revolution succeeding Revolution, one ambitious
Chief rebelling against and upsetting another". The only result is
confusion and anarchy. Macdonell ended this section of his address,
curiously, with a series of testimonials to the good character of the
Irish by English Protestants. In his conclusion, he assured the Irish
Catholics that ". . . in no class of Her Majesty's subjects in Upper
Canada, does his Excellency, our present just and impartial Lieutenant
Governor, Sir George Arthur, repose more trust and confidence than in
Catholics". This was made evident by the number of Catholics appointed
to military commands and to "other situations of high trust and honor".[48]
He did not, of course, mention the fact that almost none of these

---

[48] Ibid., as are all intervening quotations.

appointments went to Irish Catholics.

It was a remarkable performance; and the Bishop was well pleased with himself. He sent copies of both addresses to many of his correspondents. To Viscount Sidmouth, whom he had not seen since 1802, he included a letter describing the occasion of his addresses to his flock, "which I am proud to say had a powerful effect upon them. The County of Glengarry alone has four regiments embodied and serving on the frontiers".[49] The Bishop sent a copy of his address to the Irish Catholics to the Lieutenant Governor, of course, and remarked, somewhat pointedly, that "The object I had in view was to make them pleased with themselves, and to encourege [sic] them to a continuance of their loyal and faithful conduct, and to assure them that by so doing they might confidently rely on the favour and protection of both the Provincial and the Home Governments".[50] Even the Grand Orange Lodge of British North America was impressed; and adopted a resolution praising ". . . the loyal declarations made by Bishop Macdonell", and hoped that his, "virtuous and loyal conduct will have the happiest effect, and be productive of the best result".[51]

---

[49]P.A.C., Macdonell Papers, Macdonell to Sidmouth, 5 February 1839, pp. 41-42.

[50]Sanderson, Arthur Papers, Macdonell to Arthur, 2 January 1839, II, p. 6. Arthur minuted the letter to his Secretary to "send a very civil reply".

[51]Proceedings of the Grand Orange Lodge of British North America, 11 January 1839; cited in Bull, op. cit., p. 10, (Brockville).

IV

The excitement over the border raids and the renewed rebellion in Lower Canada ebbed away early in 1839. Macdonell's thoughts again turned to his seminary and the projected journey to Europe. Sir George Arthur was very interested in the Bishop's plans and attempted to be as helpful as possible. When he learned that Macdonell hoped to leave in the late spring he offered his support

> Yr. Lordship, I am aware, in order to meet my anxiety to settle the Clergy Reserves Question has withdrawn any Claim on those lands which might be advanced on the part of the Catholics--hoping that a portion of the Jesuit lands to which you consider you have a claim may be appropriated to that purpose and I believe it has been your intention to proceed to England to advance that claim.
>
> At your time of life I by no means recommend your undertaking such a voyage; nevertheless, if you do determine upon it, I think the expense of your undertaking, under such circumstances ought to be defrayed by the public and I should not hesitate to have it brought under the notice of the House if you wish it.[52]

At the same time Arthur was demonstrating his attention to Macdonell's interests in other ways. The Bishop had pressed Arthur for a position for the brother of Colonel Duncan Cameron, who commanded the North York militia, and was a particular friend. The Lieutenant Governor replied that his appointment to "the important and lucrative office of Sheriff of the Niagara District is, I think, some proof that in acknowledging your valuable aid in calling forth a loyal feeling at the moment of danger I have not been unmindful of your anxiety for the welfare

---

[52]Sanderson, Arthur Papers, Arthur to Macdonell, 13 April 1839, II, p. 117.

and happiness of the Colonel's family".[53] Two days later, Arthur wrote

to Macdonell again, informing that since he had expressed an interest

in the advancement of Alexander Macdonell (Inch) of Glengarry,". . .

supposes that he will be gratified to hear that Mr. MacDonell has

been appointed collector at Maria Town a Port of Entry on the St.

Lawrence recently established".[54]

While Macdonell may very well have been gratified by Arthur's

willingness to follow his patronage recommendations, he did not wish to

be trapped on the question of a share in the Clergy Reserves. He was

willing enough to bargain privately if there was a possibility of secur-

ing a portion of the Jesuit Estates. But he had no intention of publicly

abandoning a claim to government support from the resources of Upper

Canada. He determined, therefore, to operate on two levels. In March,

he sent a formal petition to the House of Assembly of Upper Canada on

behalf of himself, his clergy and "eighty-six thousand five hundred

Catholics of the Province".[55] He claimed an equal right to a share

in the Reserves with any other denomination in Upper Canada. The usual

justification of good conduct, loyalty and military service was advanced,

but some new reasons were also offered. The Catholic Clergy of Upper

Canada had foregone "what is their just and lawful due, for fear of

exciting discontent and disaffection", because of "the utter abhorence

---

[53] Ibid.

[54] P.A.C., RG 7, G16A, Provincial Secretary's Office, Vol. 4,
Arthur to Macdonell, Private, 15 April 1939.

[55] A printed copy of the petition is in A.A.K., Macdonell Papers.

of the Irish Emigrants to the obnoxious and oppressive tribute of
Tithes". Some compensation should be made for this patriotic for-
bearance. In a more direct vein, Macdonell reminded the Members that
it was to "the uncommon exertions of the Catholics during the last
general Election they owe their seats in the present Parliament . . ."[56]
Perhaps, the Bishop was now too old and too determined for delicacy.

The petition was referred to a committee of the House chaired
by Ogle Gowan, the rising star of the Orangemen. The report of the
committee expressed the concurrence of the members with the Bishop's
arguments, but abstained from recommending any allotment or appropriation
from the Clergy Reserves. Rather, the committee strongly urged that
the Assembly petition the Queen to grant the desired funds from "the
Jesuit Estates in Lower Canada, or from such other sources which may
seem expedient and proper".[57] In other words, while Macdonell received
a sympathetic hearing, the members had no desire to delay the Clergy
Reserve issue any further, in the hope that it was finally near resolution.
The conservative majority in the House narrowly put through a bill directing that money from the Reserves be used for religious purposes in a
manner to be determined by the British Parliament. If Macdonell was
disappointed at this ambivalence, he did not indicate it. He may very
well have expected to share in any re-allocation that Parliament might
authorize.

---

[56] Ibid., as are intervening citations.

[57] Committee Report reprinted in Corbett, op. cit., pp. 36-37.

The Bishop, meanwhile, was developing his other alternative. He was quite aware that any successful attempt by him to secure revenue from the Jesuit Estates would need powerful assistance. He had felt he could rely on his cousin, the Colonial Secretary, to support him, but Glenelg's influence with the government was ended. In order to strengthen his position, however, Macdonell sought aid in a quarter he had formerly condemned. In May, he wrote a long letter, enclosing his memorial, to Daniel O'Connell. It was filled with praise of O'Connell's success in forwarding Catholic interests in Ireland and "every part of the British Dominions".[58] He informed O'Connell that he was seeking help for the church in Upper Canada from the Jesuit Estates; and "the Catholics of this Province" were persuaded that "you [will] extend your powerful protection to Upper Canada".[59] A second solicitation for O'Connell's assistance followed in May, in which Macdonell informed him that he was coming to England immediately to apply personally at the Colonial Office. O'Connell, in fact, did try to lend his support. But he chose not to follow Macdonell's tactics, and, instead, wrote Normanby, the new Colonial Secretary, that

> I can not avoid saying that the Catholics of Upper Canada
> have strong claims on the British Government. But I
> should conceive that the best mode of satisfying their
> claims would be out of the Clergy Reserves which ought
> to be deemed public property to be used for the good of all.[60]

---

[58] A.A.K., Macdonell Papers, Macdonell to O'Connell, 23 March 1839.

[59] Ibid.

[60] P.A.C., CO42, Vol. 476, O'Connell to Normanby, 9 July 1839.

O'Connell was not proving to be much comfort.

To ensure that he would be received at the Colonial Office, Macdonell wished to be employed officially on behalf of the province in some capacity. He went to Toronto in April to see Sir George Arthur and discuss with him the question of emigration. Macdonell proposed that he should tour Ireland and Scotland on a recruiting campaign to direct settlers to Upper Canada. Recapitulating the interview in a note to the Lieutenant Governor, the Bishop requested a document for the Colonial Secretary outlining the advantages and terms he would be author-ized to extend to potential emigrants.[61] In a subsequent letter, he reminded Arthur of his offer to recommend that the province "defray the expenses of my Mission undertaken principally for the good of the Province. If such aid, however moderate, were given I could take Dr. Thomas Rolf [sic] with me whose energy and eloquence could not fail to have a power-ful effect on the intended emigrants".[62]

The Lieutenant Governor was quite receptive to Macdonell's overture; not only on its merits, but because it provided an excellent entreé to the government through which the Bishop could pursue his search for funds for his seminary. Arthur replied encouragingly.

> At your advanced age, I should not forgive myself if I
> were, in any respect, to encourage so serious an under-
> taking; but, understanding that there are important matters
> which require your personal attention in England, and that

---

[61] Sanderson, Arthur Papers, Macdonell to Arthur, 22 April 1839, II, p. 124.

[62] Ibid., Macdonell to Arthur, 3 May 1839, II, p. 143. Dr. Thomas Rolph of Ancaster was an Emigrant Agent, and a close friend of the Bishop. It may be presumed that Arthur agreed since Rolph did accompany Macdonell to Europe.

your mind is quite made up to the Expedition, I cannot
hesitate to express the opinion that there is no cause
of more vital importance than a healthy Colonisation
from the United Kingdom, and your Lordship's former great
success in this way has proved so eminently advantageous
to the Country, that I shall rejoice to hear that you
have health and strength for another encounter of the
same kind.

Arthur made a point, however, of indicating his lack of enthusiasm for

pauper emigration, but suggested that he would welcome a thousand

families. "There is a tract of country in the Western District where

a Settlement of Loyal Men would be of the greatest benefit to the

Country."[63]

With these arrangements made, Macdonell busied himself with the

final preparations for his departure. He does not seem to have taken

any part in the bitter debate raging throughout the Province on the

merits of Lord Durham's proposals for the future government of the two

Canadas. Conservatives, generally, were shocked by Durham's inaccurate

description of Upper Canadian politics, and his unfairness to those

who had been its leaders. But Durham's prestige, and the vigour of the

revived Reform Party which chose Durham as its patron, cast a pall of

gloom over many prominent Tories. Even those who had opposed Bishop

Macdonell in the past, were gropingly trying to adapt to a new era.

John Macaulay, for example, now the Civil Secretary wrote unhappily to

his mother, that "As the principle of a national church has been

abandoned, we must only now look to worldly policy and in that view I

---

[63]Ibid., Arthur to Macdonell, 5 June 1839, II, p. 161.

am for continuing to the Roman Catholic Bishop the £500 he now gets from the Crown".[64] Tories, it is supposed, must now look for solace where they could find it. Kindred spirits were hard to find.

The Bishop had two rather pleasant duties to perform before he sailed for England. On the 29 May, 1839, the Celtic Society of Upper Canada honoured him with a farewell dinner in Kingston, "furnished in Carmino's best style". The toast to Macdonell was given by the Sheriff of Kingston, and "the enthusiastic and rapturous cheering which followed defies description, it was renewed again and again".[65] It was a sentimental evening for the aging Bishop as he talked of his hopes for his forthcoming journey, but it was his "expectation to return to Kingston as soon as I can, and to spend my few remaining days among friends. . . ."[66]

A few days later Macdonell officiated at a ceremony occasioned as much by presumption and faith as by any certainty of execution. He laid the cornerstone of his seminary, Regiopolis College, on land donated by himself.[67] What funds he had been able to gather were left to aid in the construction while he went off to England to collect more.

Immediately afterward, he left Kingston for Montreal where he

---

[64] O.A., Macaulay Papers, Envelope 72, Macaulay to Ann Macaulay, 5 May 1839.

[65] An account of the dinner was given in Kingston Chronicle, 1 June 1839; see also Corbett, op. cit., pp. 38-46.

[66] Ibid.

[67] Kingston Chronicle, 12 June 1839.

visited with Bishop Lartigue.[68]   On 20 June, he sailed for England.

---

[68]R.A.Q., 1945-46, Correspondence of Lartigue, Lartigue to Bourget, 20 June 1839, pp. 104-05.

CHAPTER VII

CONCLUSION

I

When the Bishop arrived in England in mid-summer of 1839, he went

directly to London to begin his suit at the Colonial Office. In reality,

there was little prospect of success, either in securing a portion of

the Clergy Reserves of Upper Canada or in participating in the Jesuit

Estates of the lower province. The Reserves question had plagued the

Colonial Office for years. It was now, hopefully, in the process of

solution. The new Governor General, the capable and energetic Charles

Poulett Thompson, would soon propose a measure for distribution to the

legislature of Upper Canada. It was highly unlikely, as well, that the

Colonial Office would intercede for Macdonell in the tangled affairs of

the Jesuit Estates. It would be another fifty years, in fact, before

that problem was resolved, and then only painfully.

Macdonell was only one well known Upper Canadian in London that

summer. John Beverley Robinson, the Chief Justice, was there; so also

was Bishop John Strachan, wearing his new dignity happily. They all had

business of one sort or another at the Colonial Office, as Robinson in-

formed Sir George Arthur; "I saw Bishop McDonell yesterday--and the Bishop

of Toronto this morning--The former is urging some application about the

Jesuit estates--but he has made no progress yet. . . ."[1] Indeed,

Macdonell received little more than a sympathetic hearing. His cousin,

Lord Glenelg, had been replaced as Colonial Secretary by Lord Normanby

in the spring of 1839. The latter remained in this position only until

early September of the same year when he was transferred to the Home

Office. As one of his last official acts he wrote evasively to Macdonell,

indicating that he was unable to extend any encouragement since such

decisions would have to be made in the Canadas.[2]

There was little inducement for the Bishop to remain in London

after this discouraging response. In accordance with his arrangements

with Sir George Arthur he set off, in early October, to survey the pro-

spects for emigration to Upper Canada. He went first to Scotland for

a brief visit and thence to Ireland where he visited the various Bishops.[3]

He contracted what appears to have been pneumonia and was confined to

bed in Dublin for two weeks. After an apparent recovery, Macdonell wrote

enthusiastically to Arthur about his schemes for Irish emigration.[4]

[1]Sanderson, Arthur Papers, J.B. Robinson to Arthur, 31 August 1839, II, p. 228.

[2]P.A.C., C042, Vol. 467, Normanby to Macdonell, 6 September 1839.

[3]Details of Macdonell's movements and activities for the last three months of his life are sketchy. Some information is available in two contemporary articles: "Death of Bishop Alexander Macdonell", The Catholic Magazine, Vol. IV, London, pp. 102-107; and "Death of the Right Reverend Doctor Macdonell", The New York Catholic Register, I, pp. 226-27.

[4]Sanderson, Arthur Papers, Macdonell to Arthur, 22 December 1839, II, pp. 360-61.

The Christmas season was spent with the Bishop's old friend Lord Gosford,
the former Governor-in-Chief of British North America. It was Macdonell's
intention to return to London to present his emigration plans to the
Colonial Office. He travelled only as far as Dumfries, Scotland, where
he suffered a relapse and died January 14, 1840.

II

When the news of Macdonell's death reached Upper Canada the
obituary notices dwelt on his personal characteristics in recording the
event. His devotion to the Crown, his tolerance and liberality of mind,
his martial reputation and his concern for the well-being of his people
and his province were all extolled.[5] Much was made of the flourishing
condition of the Catholic Church in Upper Canada under his leadership.
The natural extension, of course, was to link the two; it was the Bishop's
personal qualities which assured the progress of the Catholic community.
It followed also that the esteem in which he was held was due to his
support of the existing social and political order. That his career
in the province should elicit such glowing testimonials comes as no
surprise. But they do little to reveal the nature of the society in
which Macdonell flourished, other than to indicate the mutually sustaining
tendencies of its leadership.

Alexander Macdonell's career in Upper Canada spanned thirty-six
years, ending almost at the same time as the separate existence of the

---

[5] Kingston Chronicle and Gazette, 28 March 1840, is a good example.

province itself. With his passing, went also the political system which had come to dominate Upper Canada, especially since the close of the War of 1812. Macdonell both approved and supported that system of oligarchic leadership without which would be lost those necessary qualities of order, stability and deference, the marks of real liberty. But it is not enough to say that Macdonell was a leading conservative in a province which honoured the Loyalist tradition.

Upper Canada was a garrison state. The external threat--the levelling, irreligious, bumptious democracy of the United States--was ever present. It was not Americans that the Tories disliked and feared, but Americanism. The real problem, to paraphrase Richard Hofstadter, was not American ideology, but that America was an ideology. It both attracted and repelled Upper Canadians. The Tory élite of the province rejected it, not simply because this position was self-serving, but as a result of their conviction that republicanism led inevitably to demagoguery and anarchy. The prerequisite of true liberty was stability in their view.

The severity of the external threat as perceived by the garrison mentality meant also that internal dissent represented an inflated danger. This obtained not only in the political sphere. The integrity of the province was preserved only partially through oligarchic direction. Equally, if not more important were the agencies of social control such as the churches and education which buttressed the status quo. An O'Grady, in other words, presented nearly as critical a challenge as Mackenzie.

One other general characteristic of the Tory outlook ought also
to be mentioned. While they were conscious of the reality of their
life as British North Americans, they continued to think of themselves
as English abroad. This was not simply an affectation but a vital part
of their compensation for their "peculiar position". The connection
with the mother country, both constitutional and personal, was their
sheet-anchor. But the cable must be constantly tended lest neglect,
ignorance or wrong-headedness at the other end should suddenly cast them
adrift.

III

There is little point in avoiding the term "Family Compact" to
designate the Tory leadership which controlled Upper Canada, however
inaccurate, technically, that appellation might be. It is a useful term
to describe the political and bureaucratic élite which shared a broad
community of interest and conviction. But it should be noted that as
in most families this one also had its spats, especially on economic
questions. The long rivalry between Kingston and York/Toronto Tories
is a prime example. The familial cohesion was not always permanent;
members would sometimes stray. One might consider the fascinating career
of Henry John Boulton who began as a High Tory and ended a Clear Grit.
This is simply to indicate, however, that the Compact was not completely
homogeneous. The inner core--the Strachan--Robinson group based at the
capital--fully accepted the basic tenets. But so also did Christopher
Hagerman who emerged as the leading Tory politician of the 1830s, yet

strongly urged the economic interests of Kingston.

What occurred over the years was almost inevitable. As the population of the province increased, as its economic life became more varied and its social structure more complex, new forces emerged which demanded to be served. The Compact, in order to maintain control, had to make practical adjustments to broaden its network of support. Thus the growth, as Professor Wise has argued, of a matrix of local élites throughout Upper Canada bound to the Compact through ideology and patronage. There were also special interest groups to be accommodated, as long as they did not represent a threat to the existing leadership.

Bishop Macdonell estimated, in a petition of 1838, that there were upwards of eighty-six thousand Catholics in Upper Canada. As a cohesive group, they were, over the years, a potent political factor in the province. Since Macdonell was predisposed toward the Tories and, except on the question of establishment, shared their outlook, it was advantageous that he be recruited into the system. The stark equation of votes in return for patronage and advancement, however, does not do justice to either party. There was nothing cynical in Macdonell's attachment to conservatism. Both theologically and philosophically, his entire career bore witness. The alternative to the Tories, in Macdonell's view, was chaos. For their part, the Tories recognized in the Bishop a kindred spirit. If they were uneasy about his Catholicism, they had no doubt of his political credentials. They were not intolerant, despite Macdonell's fulminations and suspicions at times. For purely practical reasons a place could be found for him; but it went beyond

this. His social values were so like those of the Compact, his conception of Upper Canada so in tune with theirs, that the Tories felt
a natural sympathy with his aspirations. Macdonell would be a welcome
colleague in holding back the enemy at the gates.

The recruitment policy of the Compact had to reflect the changing
demography of the province. This was true, however, only to the extent
that new supporters accepted the system and added strength to it. It
did not follow that the local élites were influenced by this practice.
If Kingston is any example--and it was an important one--these local
groups could be much more exclusive and tightly-knit. Over the years
Macdonell sought preferment for his friend Walter McCuniffe, an Irish
Catholic merchant of that town. He blamed his lack of success on the
obstinacy of the Macaulay-Kirby-Markland connection which appeared to
control appointments in Kingston. Local élites could afford to be more
determinedly homogeneous since they were not subject to the same pressures
and demands as the provincial Tory leadership. It should also be
pointed out that Macdonell's influence in his own Eastern District was
almost equally strong. A non-Scot would have difficulty making his way
there. To put it another way, the lines of communication among élites
tended to be vertical.

In seeking the material advantage of Catholic leaders and his
pople as a whole Macdonell had two objectives in mind. He was shrewd
enough to realize that political allegiance depended to a large extent
on economic matters. It was necessary to demonstrate that within the
system he helped to sustain, Catholics would have the opportunity to

prosper; thus his continuing attention to land grants and positions in government service. On a larger scale, given the inevitable comparison with the United States, Upper Canada must hold out fair prospects. The Tories, as a group, were vitally interested in economic growth and encouraged it. Macdonell revealed the same spirit in his persistent interest in emigration and settlement schemes. It was important to Macdonell as well that the government place a high value on Catholic support. Preferment to Catholics and subventions to the church of various kinds would confirm its acceptance and respectability in the province.

Macdonell's role in the politics of Upper Canada can be best seen, perhaps, in his long and sometimes difficult relationship with John Strachan. The Archdeacon, of course, was at the centre of activity and the Bishop on the periphery, yet their careers were often intertwined as we have seen. They continually saw each other as rivals especially in the early years; a condition that was exacerbated somewhat as the Catholic population outstripped that of the Church of England. The bedeviling question of establishment, with its subsidiary problem of the Clergy Reserves, divided them. As men of affairs, however, they saw practical advantages in an amicable connection. As the years passed and political tension in the province heightened they came to realize that they had much in common. It was no longer simply a matter of trading off advantages. Both men were products of the British counter-revolutionary spirit of the close of the eighteenth century. As such they shared a deep commitment to order and stability. This does not mean they were inflexible and static. But they conceived of progress as organic change, a process of gaining the future by building on the past.

They were both leaders of hierarchically structured churches, the social implications of which can best be summed up in the word deference--the reciprocal duty of one class to another. In a later time this would be called paternalism or worse and found objectionable. But the alternative, to Strachan and Macdonell, lay just across Lake Ontario. While they disagreed on the practical question of church establishment, neither of them would question the theory of social utility which it involved. Nor did they differ on the function of education, or the need to free their clergy from a too-close dependence on their congregations. While they could never completely give themselves to each other, their natural sympathies and shared convictions bound them closer together.

The career of Alexander Macdonell in the public life of Upper Canada thus demonstrates both the strength and weakness of the oligarchic rule of the Family Compact. The Tory élite tried to adjust to the changing character and aspirations of the province. A Macdonell could be recruited, but was he really so different, after all? There is now a greater appreciation of the hopes and aspirations of Upper Canada's Tories. But it must be conceded that they held an overly narrow view of the range of possibilities open to them; and they became in the end irrelevant. As for Macdonell, he has already a secure place in Canadian Catholic hagiography. It is hoped that a further dimension has now been added.

A NOTE ON THE AUTHOR

James Edgar Rea was born in Kingston, Ontario and attended the University of Manitoba and Queen's University after serving for six years as a Flying Officer in the Royal Canadian Air Force.

He has published a number of articles on Upper Canadian and Western Canadian history and The Winnipeg General Strike (Toronto, 1973).

He is presently Associate Professor of History at the University of Manitoba.

Bishop Alexander Macdonell and the Politics of Upper Canada was written originally as a doctoral thesis at Queen's University.